Mo

MENDIP WALKS

TWELVE CIRCULAR WALKS OF DISCOVERY

Sue Gearing

HALSGROVE

First published in Great Britain in 2004
Reprinted 2005

Copyright © 2004 Sue Gearing

British Library Cataloguing-in-Publication Data
A CIP record for this title is available from the British Library

ISBN 1 84114 363 4

HALSGROVE
Halsgrove House
Lower Moor Way
Tiverton, Devon EX16 6SS
Tel: 01884 243242
Fax: 01884 243325
email: sales@halsgrove.com
website: www.halsgrove.com

Printed and bound by The Cromwell Press, Trowbridge

CONTENTS

The Walks
(all circular and all have a pub en route, except for walk 8)
Time given is walking time only. Allow for stopping, looking, refreshment etc.

❧

Les Davies, Mendip Warden, looking across at the Area of Outstanding Natural Beauty – the west Mendip ridge – from Prospect Stile near Hinton Blewett.

Sue and Shabba standing by the stocks on the green at Faulkland.

❧

*I would like to dedicate this book to my dear
dad, Bill Taylor who died during the period of
researching, walking and writing. He set me off
on my love of walking as a child and would have
been proud of this second Mendip 'challenge'.
I seem to have been walking all my life and have
clocked up more than 350 published circular
walks in the West Country. Many of these are
part of my weekly walk in* West Country Life, *
the colour supplement of the* Western Daily Press.

❧

Acknowledgements

These twelve circles have been made so much easier and more pleasant thanks to Les Davies, Senior Warden of the AONB Service who willingly helped with factual information, advice and clarification of footpaths.

My thanks also to those many other people who contributed information, and in particular, the volunteer Mendip Rangers who checked the circles before publication and gave helpful advice and suggestions. I admire the patience and determination of my walking friends, Jane, Pauline, Irene and Jackie, and of course to my husband, Peter. When I walked alone, I was accompanied very enthusiastically by Shabba, a friend's dog who has taken over as my companion from Jessie, sadly now deceased. He found the walks full of interesting smells... I expect you may enjoy the walks for other reasons! I certainly hope so.

The 'Hill Wise' Guide to enjoying the Mendip Hills

It is a pleasure to welcome you to Sue Gearing's second book about walking on the Mendip Hills. Mendip for me is a very special place, and I hope that through this book you will be able to find and enjoy the unique and special qualities this area has to offer.

The countryside we all enjoy and strive to protect today has been generations in its shaping. It has changed over the years, and will continue to evolve as our requirements on this landscape change with it. After all, change is a natural process and we cannot 'pickle' the natural environment and put it in a jar, but we can hope to conserve those very special bits for future generations to enjoy.

This is a working landscape, inhabited by people and grazed by livestock, so some care and courtesy is needed when visiting. Contrary to popular myth, farmers and landowners will be pleased to see you enjoying your time in the countryside, if you treat it with respect. Remember they will be earning their livelihood from this land and will not be pleased about damaged crops or gates that are left open allowing livestock to wander. Please remember that a dog on a lead is definitely under control, whereas one off the lead can be questionable no matter how well trained it may be. Livestock do frighten easily, so keep your dog close at all times.

Please take care of yourself as well. The Mendip climate can be somewhat changeable, even in the summer months and during the winter in becomes downright hostile. Go equipped for bad weather and you wont go far wrong. Wear good boots, take a waterproof and spare clothing to put on if the temperature drops.

During the summer in particular, wear socks and cover your arms and legs when walking through bracken or undergrowth to lessen the chance of picking up ticks. Check your self and your dog at regular intervals, and at the end of the day. A free leaflet is available from the AONB Service at Charterhouse on request; just send us a stamped addressed envelope.

Don't forget to let someone know where you are going and what time you expect to be back. This could help us get to you quickly in the unfortunate event of an accident whilst you are out walking. Remember that if you have to use your mobile phone in an emergency, that your call could go anywhere in the UK. Please be as precise about your location as you can, as those taking your call may not know the area.

Park your car sensibly. Please do not obstruct farm gateways or residential entrances. Use the car parks wherever possible and remember there is safety in numbers. Don't be tempted to park in isolated areas; the thieves know all the good spots to visit where they can break into visitors' cars. Don't let them do it to you, take any valuables with you and don't leave anything on view, even an empty bag is worth a go as far as the thief is concerned. If you see anything suspicious, get a car registration number if you can and let the police know what you saw and where.

If you find a blocked footpath or some other obstruction do not attempt to remedy the problem yourself. Actions such as cutting wire will only worsen the situation and lead to resentment and anger. Report the problem to your local Public Rights of Way Officer from the Council, they are the ones who can sort the situation out. Never climb over fences or walls. Apart from the risk of injury to yourself, there is the real risk of damage to property that will not endear you to the local farming population.

Do not be tempted to explore caves or ruined buildings you may come across. If you would like to find out what Mendip below ground is like, contact your local caving club who will be glad to help, or contact the AONB Service who will put you in touch with them.

During the warm summer days Mendip's snake population can be active. Adders are not aggressive creatures, and like most of us, only want a quiet life. Be aware that they are about and that they like to bask on walls and sunny banks, treat all snakes with respect. Leave the wildlife alone and it won't bother you.

Camping and open fires are not permitted without the landowner's consent. On Burrington Commons (Black Down and Burrington Ham), they are not permitted at all. Neither are they allowed in any of the Forest areas.

Remember that you will need to be responsible for your own actions and well being. The walks in this book are not mountainous, but you will need to be realistic about your own capabilities and level of fitness as the walks can be challenging at times. Finally, enjoy yourself. Make the most of your time on the Hill and take away pleasant memories of your visit here. I do, after all, want you to come back again.

Les Davies
Senior Warden
Mendip Hills Area of Outstanding Natural Beauty, (AONB)

MAP SHOWING APPROXIMATE LOCATION OF WALKS

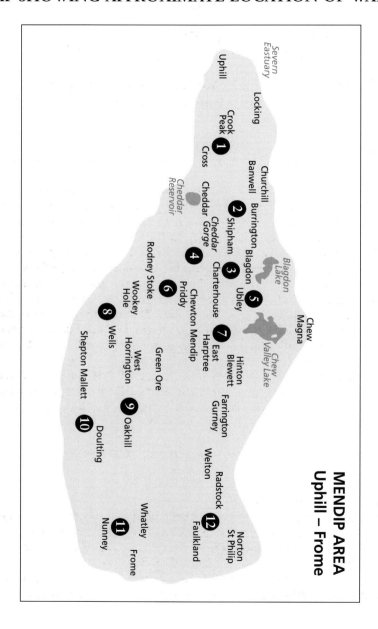

Peak of Perfection

Compton Bishop – Crook Peak – Wavering Down – Cross – Compton Bishop

Distance: About 6 miles.
Duration: Approx three and a half hours walking.
Map: OS Explorer Map 153. Weston-super-Mare. Reference: 393 549

On a sunny clear day, few walks could surpass this one for breath-taking vistas on all sides and bracing air. Wear good boots and windproof gear as the going could be slippery after rain and up on top it can be very windy. This circle goes past, and up to the top as well if you wish, the only pointed hill on Mendip, Crook Peak. It is a stunning National Trust area, and together with adjoining Wavering Down, offers many wildflowers and much bird life. There is a good deal of uphill walking, some quite steep but many sections are well graded and there are long flat stretches and some fairly steep downhill work, too. For refreshment there are two coaching inns in Cross to choose from and then comes a flat riverside walk plus a short steepish climb to return to the start.

The walk begins from a parking lay-by on the Cross to Webbington and Bleadon road. From the A38 near Axbridge turn right at Cross along a quiet lane to Compton Bishop. The lay-by is about 1.5 miles along on the left and is ringed by low wooden posts.

Across the road are three gates leading onto the National Trust land of Crook Peak.

START – *Alternative starts:*
A If you are feeling energetic and want a steep, short scramble to get you quickly up to the ridge take the left hand gate and scramble steeply straight up for about six minutes until you reach a grassy ridge and a steep drop on the other side. Turn left and follow instructions from *
B For a gentler ascent – but still quite a climb – take the right hand gate. The path parallels the road for a short distance climbing gently. At a

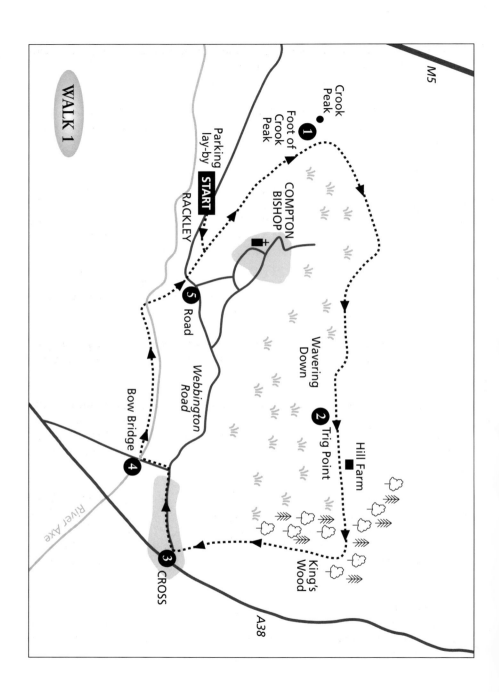

WALK 1

M5

Crook Peak

Foot of Crook Peak ①

COMPTON BISHOP

Parking lay-by

START

RACKLEY

⑤ Road

Webbington Road

Wavering Down

② Trig Point

Hill Farm

Bow Bridge

④

River Axe

③ CROSS

King's Wood

A38

clearing and junction of paths, go up left through a wooden barrier and start to climb more steeply on a path which goes along the ridge.
* Continue to climb up towards rocky Crook Peak.

Down on the right is the village of Compton Bishop nestling in the shadow of the hills. Its name comes from the fact that it was owned by the Bishop of Bath and Wells until the fifteenth century.

1   FOOT OF CROOK PEAK
The path skirts to the right of and below the Peak but it is worth going up on the top for the best views of all. Take care as it can be very windy up here. The Somerset Levels, Exmoor, Wales and the Black Mountains can all be clearly seen from here as well as Winscombe and the end of the Mendip chain, Brean Down, Steep Holm and Flat Holm islands.

The Peak's distinctive shape was used for centuries as a guide by shipping in the difficult waters of the Bristol Channel, and was one of the great beacons which warned of the approach of the Spanish Armada.

After going up, drop down onto the path below. If you don't go up, just stay on the path which heads across to Wavering Down and a Mendip dry stone wall.

The wall which runs along much of the Down is the ancient Saxon boundary and now the county boundary between North Somerset and Somerset. Volunteers with the National Trust have been working on this wall for years. A total of 1032 yards of walling was rebuilt between 1988 and 2003, and topped out in April 2003 with a commemorative stone.

Turn right with the wall on your left and you are now going east on the West Mendip Way, the 32 miles long distance path from Uphill to Wells. Follow this wide track/grassy swathe for nearly 2 miles, following wall or fence, with amazing views in all directions if visibility is half way reasonable.
The track climbs up quite steeply to the summit of Wavering Down to the trig point at 211 metres.

2   TRIG POINT
The path starts to drop down and there may well be alternative footpath routes to take you down, avoiding the slippery more muddy bridleway. On the left you pass Hill Farm.

Dropping down on the west Mendip Way by Hill Farm.

This sheltered spot has been used for stock keeping for centuries and was formerly known as Eames fold, but is now a private house.

At Hill Farm make your way over in the direction of the wall again if you are not already there and continue on down. Just as you are about to enter King's Wood ahead, bear right with the woodland on your left. The path then goes into the woodland.

This ancient area has many small leaved lime trees some of which may be four hundred years old.

The way through is not very well defined, but continue down through the woodland. Reach a fence ahead and crossing bridleway. Turn right on this, still in woodland. Follow the bridleway signs which take you left down hill. Ignore side turns. In Spring this area was pungent with wild garlic when I walked here. At a t-junction with a broad crossing track, turn right and stay with the path. Unfortunately there is some traffic noise from the nearby A38 along here. Come out of woodland into more open land with views across the Levels again.

The path goes up and down and eventually drops down to a wooden hunting gate. Go through and continue downhill on the path which becomes rather rocky and potentially slippery – so go carefully. Reach the road in the small village of Cross.

3   CROSS

The village was formerly an important posting place with three coaching inns on the Bridgwater to Bristol road, two of which have survived. There was a quarry in the hill behind and also a brewery.

For one of the old hostelries, the New Inn, make a detour left of about 50m along the road. Or, to continue the circle, turn right and soon reach the other inn, the White Hart. There is a terraced garden up behind the White Hart. The paddock above this is the home of a friendly Gloucester Old Spot called Daisy, owned by the pub's landlord.

Legend has it that the pub is haunted by one of the victims of Judge Jefferies (the Hanging Judge) when he came to the West Country after the Monmouth Rebellion.

From the White Hart, turn right on the Webbington Road and cross over to walk along the pavement.

You can't fail to notice the interesting selection of houses in Cross including one on the right with a flamboyant display of topiary yews, some of them dating back to the 1890s. Just past this is a rare example of an 1859 wall post box with an integral hood and aperture flap.

Continue along the pavement and take the lane left to Weare and Highbridge – the old coaching road.

4   BOW BRIDGE

Cross Bow Bridge over the Axe river and immediately take the footpath on the right. Now it's a pleasant flat walk through fields with the river on your right for about a mile.

We are heading towards the tiny hamlet of Rackley (but turning off before we reach it). It developed as a port on the River Axe, following a grant from Richard I to the Bishops of Bath and Wells in 1189. Coal was imported here from South Wales and there are still photographs showing it being unloaded by hand into donkey carts.

Turn right over a single plank bridge with iron railings. Go across, diagonally left in the field, in the direction of a farm. Cross another stile and go through the field, keeping parallel but not close to the right edge. Cross a stile by a telegraph pole onto the road.

5 ROAD

Turn left with great care on this blind bend. It is not a sensible idea to walk back along the road to the car as there is no verge or path, so we are taking a footpath which runs above the road. Cross over to the other side at the Rackley Lane turn, and take the path opposite. Go through a wooden gate and then fork left, shortly going through wooden railings and follow the path quite steeply up for about three minutes, going over rocky ground and reaching a clearing. If you took the easier route at the start you will have already been to this clearing and will now retrace your steps. Turn left and follow the path which parallels the road down on the left. Come back down through a gate back to the road and the car park opposite.

🍷 The New Inn, Cross, tel: 01934 732455.
🍷 The White Hart, Cross, tel: 01934 732260.

Dolbury Delight

Shipham – Dolbury Hill Fort – Star – Shipham

Distance: About 4.25 miles.
Duration: Approx two and a quarter hours walking.
Map: OS Explorer Map 141. Cheddar Gorge and Mendip Hills West.
Reference: 445 575

For beauty, variety and great views try this short, bracing and, in parts, challenging walk in the Mendip Area of Outstanding Natural Beauty, ideal for a morning or afternoon. It takes you from a former mining village on Mendip, through woodland and then a steep climb up to the grassy top of an ancient hill fort, on a little known stepped path, before dropping down to two pubs. Then it's an easy walk back over 'gruffy ground' with great views to the hill fort or up through a bluebell and daffodil valley.

The circle begiins in Shipham, one of the few villages on the Mendip plateau, about 0.75 miles off the A38 Bristol-Exeter road, south of the traffic lights at Churchill. Park in the centre of the village, somewhere suitable and safe near the Square which is the open area opposite the Miner's Arms.
Shipham is today a pleasant residential village, a far cry from the poor and rowdy community of miners that it was in the eighteenth century. The reforming sisters Hannah and Martha More observed that they were 'savage and depraved... brutal in their natures and ferocious in their manners'. The sisters worked hard to improve the living and social conditions of the mining families. On one occasion, Hannah tried in vain to introduce twice daily prayers at the Shipham poorhouse. 'We could not get it done in Shipham for a sad reason – not one could read: but alas everyone could and did, swear.' One of the problems of upholding order and the law in the village was that the constables were too afraid to discipline or apprehend the miners, fearing for their own safety. Shipham, and Rowberrow, were important calamine mining centres from the mid sixteenth century to the mid nineteenth century, supply-ing a willing market in Bristol for the making of brass. More than 100 mines

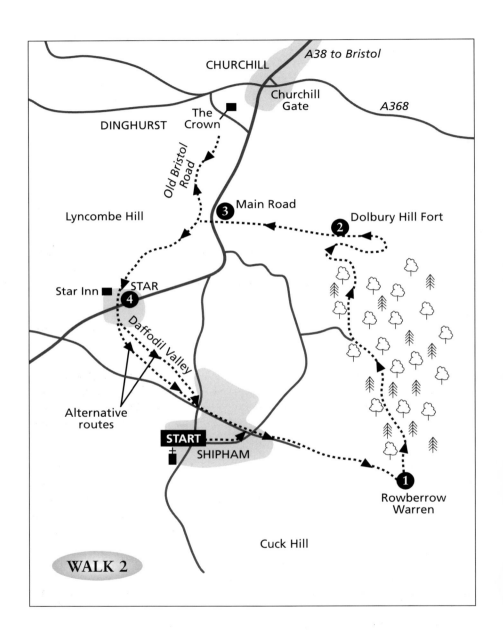

A38 to Bristol

CHURCHILL

Churchill
Gate

A368

The
Crown

DINGHURST

Old Bristol Road

Lyncombe Hill

Main Road ❸

Dolbury Hill Fort ❷

Star Inn ■ STAR ❹

Daffodil Valley

Alternative
routes

START ❶ Rowberrow
Warren

SHIPHAM

Cuck Hill

WALK 2

20

for lead and calamine (a zinc ore) were recorded in the area. Many of the houses were even built directly over mine shafts to protect the families' mining rights so they were never far away from the possibility of lead and metal poisoning.

Apart from the 'gruffy' ground around the village, (from the old English 'grafa' meaning ditch) where mining took place, the land around is rich in prehistoric remains.

START

Walk up The Hollow which is the road on the left of the green, passing on the right Lenny's Coffee Shop.

This is a friendly community café run in aid of St Leonard's church – a good place for a coffee, at least

Fork right on Barnpool. Reach a junction at a grassy triangle and turn right. Follow it all the way, gently climbing past houses. At the top go ahead on the marked path into Rowberrow Warren woods.

1   ROWBERROW WARREN

The stony track drops downhill. Reach a junction at the bottom by a Bristol Water enclosure.

The crossing path was the route taken by miners from Shipham and Rowberrow in the latter part of the nineteenth century when mining for lead and calamine in their area had ceased and they sought work at the mineries at Charterhouse. The path which went up across Black Down became known as the Slaggers Path.

Don't cross the stream, but instead turn left on the bridleway to Rowberrow following the stream on your right. Ignore any side turns. Just stay along the bottom passing two or three pretty country cottages on your right. Ignore the tarmac lane which forks up left to Rowberrow. Just keep ahead, passing close to a cottage, and then through a metal gate. Pass a stable and come again into woodland.

When you reach a t-junction with a track, turn left. After a couple of minutes at a point where the tree canopy is not so thick, take a stile on the right which is somewhat hidden in the trees. Here is the National Trust Dolbury Warren sign and the steep bank of Dolbury Hill fort ahead (don't worry you are not going straight up!).

The Warren is a Site of Special Scientific Interest, rich with grassland flowers such as orchids, yellow wort, drop wort and kidney vetch and at least 30 species of butterflies.

Bear right on a small path through the woodland and keep ahead, going gradually over to the left to the bottom of the steep slope. Follow the path gently up and it becomes steeper and steeper and then stepped and out onto the grassy slope itself. Look back at the great view over the valley as you go with the church and old manor of Rowberrow nestling amongst the trees. At the top follow the path along the edge of the escarpment with the steep drop on your left. Ignore a stile on the right, just keep along the edge for about a couple of minutes until you come up to the outer bank of the hill fort.

2   DOLBURY HILL FORT

It is a Scheduled Ancient Monument and Site of Special Scientific Interest and one of the most beautiful strategic vantage points on the Mendip escarpment. We want to go further into the middle of the fort rather than on this southern edge, so go right up along the bank on a small path. Go over a crossing path and keep on up on the bank, still climbing. At the next small crossing path turn left over the bank, ditch and other outer bank and into the fort.

On the path below Dolbury Hill Fort.

The name dol means a moor and burg a fortress. This is the eastern end which was probably the weakest, hence the double bank. It is said to be an Iron Age hill fort although little excavation work has been carried out. However, Roman and Saxon coins, spearheads and swords have been found. The fort also did service as a rabbit warren providing food for the local people. You may pass the ruins of the keeper's cottage on the highest ground within the fort.

Stay in this direction walking down the centre of Dolbury looking along towards the Severn estuary.
If you go a little more to the right you come into the middle proper with the best views.

On a clear day the views take in the Welsh coast and hills, including the Sugar Loaf, down the Mendip spine to Brean Down, Steep Holm and Flat Holm and over Wrington Vale as well as down to the Quantocks and Exmoor. It is a great place to view the village of Wrington in Wrington Vale to the north, sheltering below the hills and to see the glorious church tower. It is said that the striking Victoria Tower on the Houses in Parliament at Westminster was modelled on Wrington's church tower.

Drop down through the grassy centre of the fort and out through the western 'gate'. Here there is quite a lot of noise from the A38 – the sound bounces back from the rocks below. The stony path bends left and winds downhill. Go through a hunting gate and on down. Turn right on the tarmac lane down through the hamlet of Dolbury Bottom to the busy A38.

3 MAIN ROAD
Cross with care and follow the stony bridleway on the other side, uphill. At the top reach a junction with a track which was the old Bristol Road. Our circle continues by going left, but for the renowned cottage pub, the Crown Inn, turn right for a few minutes on the track and then return to this point. The Crown serves reasonably priced, quality snacks and has an intimate, old-time pub atmosphere.

It is situated in the former hamlet of Dinghurst – known as Thinghurst in 1290 – near which there was an old turnpike on the Bristol Road, known as Churchill Gate.

Follow the track uphill looking across to Lyncombe Hill. Ignore side paths and at a Bristol Water enclosure, keep straight ahead on the track going downhill all the way to the hamlet of Star and the A38 again.

4 STAR
Turn right to the Star Inn, another popular pub that has served travellers over many years. It may not serve snack lunches every day so ring and check. Go past the Star and then cross the A38 and go up Cheddarcombe. Pass a line of old miners' cottages on the right. Here you have a choice of routes back to Shipham:

1 The first is gently up a stony bridleway through Cheddarcombe – known locally as Daffodil Valley – and in spring you may prefer this walk and hope to see daffodils and bluebells. For this, just keep straight

on – don't go left over the stile into the field. The track continues along and eventually comes up by a cottage. Go out onto the tarmac and up to Broadway and then on to the main road. Turn right back to where you began.

2 For a more open route, turn left by the miners' cottages over a stile into the field. Go ahead parallel with the left fence for about 60 yards and then bear up right onto a bank, passing to the left of a fence, sealing off an old mine entrance. Continue on uphill passing to the left of a telegraph pole. Here you can see Dolbury Fort very clearly. Walk parallel with the trees over on the right. Pass under the power lines and go through a rough football field, drawing closer to the trees on the right. At the top of the field, turn right and follow the path out, past derelict buildings, and out to the main road, over a stone slab stile.

When the road was being turnpiked in 1827, a great deal of work had to be carried out to build up across Cheddarcombe and this included quarrying out stone from Cuck Hill on the other side of the village

Turn right past a turnpike cottage.

❧ The Crown, Churchill, tel: 01934 852995.
❧ The Star Inn, tel: 01934 842569.

Valley View

Charterhouse – Hazel Manor –
Compton Martin (optional) – Charterhouse

Distance: 7.5 miles or 6.25 miles.
Duration: Approx four hours or three and a quarter hours walking.
Map: OS Explorer Map 141. Cheddar Gorge and Mendip Hills West.
Reference: 506 555.

*Here is a chance to enjoy a really spectacular view of Chew Valley Lake
and the hills around, and to walk through an emerging mixed forest
planted on Mendip a few years ago. It is easy walking on tracks, footpaths and quiet lanes and if you choose the short route, there are virtually
no hills. If you do go down to Chewton Mendip to enjoy refreshment at
the very popular Ring O' Bells, then it will add about another 1.25 miles
of beautiful woodland walking downhill and then up. The uphill starts
steeply but then becomes very reasonable and in my book it is worth
doing the full circle. We also pass close by some fascinating industrial
history. This walk can be accessed either by car or by bus.
Wear boots or good footwear, as usual.*

*Go to Charterhouse up on Mendip. Take the B3134 road across Mendip
About a mile from the top of Burrington Combe turn right towards
Charterhouse. After about another mile turn left down a small lane at the side
of Charterhouse Centre and head for the small parking area down the bottom
by an interpretation board about the Romans on Mendip. An Explorer bus
service from Bristol to Cheddar stops at Charterhouse Centre. * Get off at the
centre, turn down the lane at the side and walk down to the car park and
interpretation board.*

START

From the parking area, take the main track along, shortly going through
a metal barrier across the track. Continue on and look out for the first
public footpath arrow going left. Follow this narrow path down towards
a pond.

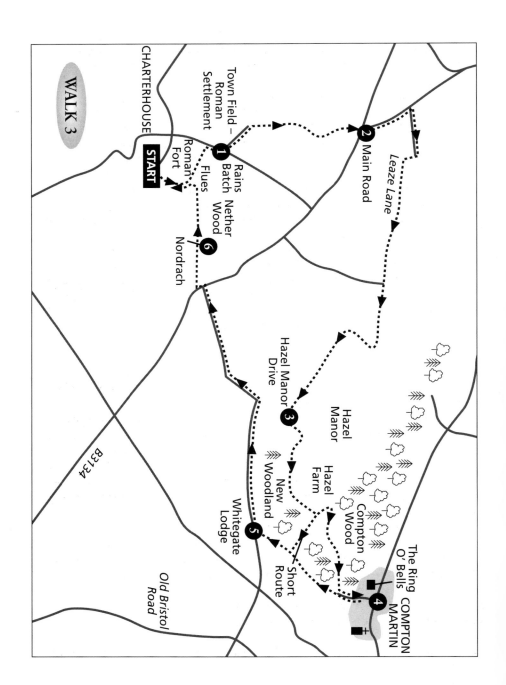

WALK 3

CHARTERHOUSE

Town Field –
Roman
Settlement

Rains
Batch

START

Roman
Fort

Nether
Wood

Flues

Nordrach

Main Road

Leaze Lane

Hazel Manor
Drive

Hazel
Manor

New
Woodland

Hazel
Farm

Compton
Wood

Whitegate
Lodge

Short
Route

The Ring
O' Bells

COMPTON
MARTIN

B3134

Old Bristol
Road

26

The pond is a rarity on Mendip because in limestone areas the water seeps down through, but here there is a skin of clay and shale on the ground to act as a water-proof layer.

Notice the black slag and spoil heaps around, left from the reworking of lead waste here in the mid nineteenth century. The promise of lead and silver on Mendip was one reason for the Romans coming to Britain and Charterhouse became an important mining centre under them, but mining probably took place here before their arrival. The Romans are believed to have mined there from about AD49. The earliest known lead 'pig' in Britain was produced at Charterhouse. Mendip lead was exported by the Romans – some having being found at Pompeii and it is thought the lead was worked by slaves and prisoners of war. Mining continued after the Romans, on and off for several centuries, before ceasing altogether. The bumpy ground you see here, known as 'gruffy ground' is the remains of mining activity. In the nineteenth century, using new skills of extraction learned from the tin miners in Cornwall, a lead re-smelting industry sprang up at four centres on Mendip including here at Charterhouse. A furnace, buddle pits for washing the old slag, and flues were constructed, linked into the natural ponds. We see the old flues later in the walk. You may be able to spot some of the large blocks of slag in the shape of the trolleys they filled when they came out of the furnace.

Pass to the left of the pond.

This pond helped to provide water to the round pits, 'buddle pits' where the lead slag was washed prior to resmelting.

The whole of this area is part of Blackmoor Nature owned and managed by Somerset County Council as an area of recreation and as an educational resource. Parties of schoolchildren stay at Charterhouse Centre and learn much about flora and fauna in the Reserve. You may well see them pond dipping and roaming around the Reserve looking for particular species of plant and wildlife. Much of the area is a Site of Special Scientific Interest because of the richness of wildlife on land and in the ponds Some of the plants in this area are particularly associated with lead – alpine penny cress and spring sandwort and there are many species of butterflies. It is also a good place to spot buzzards, kestrels and mammals such as fox, badger, hare, stoat, weasel and roe deer. Adders and lizards also enjoy sunny spots in the dry grassland and on the walls.

Reach a stile which brings you into a field.
Walk up the left side and cross a stile onto the road.

On the other side of the road is Town Field, the site of an early Roman settlement.

Blackmoor Nature Reserve in snow.

1 RAINS BATCH

Turn right and shortly take the first lane on the left. This is Rains Batch. Follow it steadily uphill, passing a bungalow on the left.

> *Further up the hill on the left in a field is the site of a small Roman amphitheatre, probably used for meetings as it was not larger enough for lavish sporting events.*
>
> *There are good views unfolding, across to the top of Cheddar Gorge and back across the slag and gruffy ground. Beyond this on the horizon are the Bronze Age burial mounds of Ashen Hill and Priddy Nine Barrows and ahead rises Black Down, the highest area of Mendip, topped by more Bronze Age barrows, called Beacon Batch.*

Cross a marked stile on the right and go diagonally across the field, keeping fairly well over to the left and heading for the far left corner where you cross a stile. Go ahead and cross another stile in the hedge and then follow the left edge of the field and go ahead into another field. Continue on heading for the far left corner and staying close to the left edge. Keep on in the next field in the same direction and climb gently up, passing a farmhouse on your left and reaching the B3134 road.

2 MAIN ROAD

Turn left for a few yards, cross and turn right down the Blagdon road. Already you should be getting some of the first views over Chew Valley and across west to Weston-super-Mare and beyond. Take the first lane on the right – Leaze Lane and enjoy the vistas over the lake as you go along. By the farm, turn right up a grassy track marked as a footpath and at the corner follow it round to the left (ignore the stile ahead). Follow the track along to a stile, cross and then continue on as before in the same direction along the left edge of the field. Cross a stile and go across a lane and follow the track ahead still going east.

Keep on and go through a hunting gate by a big gate and continue on as before. Follow the track round a right hand bend and then walk under a line of magnificent beeches. Cross a stile by a gate and go left along a grassy track, walking alongside some of the new forest.

A notice explains something about the extent and nature of the 500 acre Hazel Manor Woodland which is a project of the Will Woodland Trust. The first phase is now well underway and you can see the amount of work involved not only in planting but also to fence the area against deer, to leave buffer zones for fence inspection and to allow good access to the new woodland.

Go over another stile by a gate and continue on along the track, passing a copse on the left. At the end go over a stile by a main gate and reach the drive to Hazel Manor, fringed with beeches.

3 HAZEL MANOR DRIVE

Hazel Manor was once one of Mendip's large houses – a nineteenth century hunting lodge – which sadly was burned down in the 1920s and nothing visible remains of it, save for the long drive. There is today a house called Hazel Manor, but it is a farm and not even on the site of the old manor. There is also Hazel Farm.

Turn left through a large hunting gate and along the drive for a very short distance.

After the fourth beech on the right, turn right across the grass at the side and through an opening in the hedge. Here a notice explains that this is a permissive path through the new woodland. Follow the mown track and orange topped posts for about ¾ of a mile through different sections of the new woodland by which time you are heading north again and looking straight over the valley and Chew Valley Lake. Leave the woodland over a stile by a gate and come onto a grassy track. Here the views are stupendous given a clear day. Over to your left is Hazel Farm.

For the shorter route: turn right along the grassy track with the valley and lake down on your left. Eventually go right into another field and just continue on in the same direction as before with the wall on your left. Go through another large hunting gate and turn right following the yellow footpath arrows with woodland dropping down on the left and wire fence on the right. Near a right hand bend join the longer route coming up from the woods and now just follow the route from ✦.

For the full route down to Compton Martin: turn left along the grassy track and at the gate to the Farm, don't go through, but instead turn right alongside the wall and shortly bear away to the right going downhill towards the wooded slopes of the hill. Reach another large hunting gate and go through into the woodland. Now follow the track downhill quite steeply through Compton Wood a haven for wild flowers and birds. Go through a gate and continue through the wood. Ignore one small path going left and continue down the path, which may be quite hard going in parts, until you reach the marked Limestone Link path going left downhill – still in the woods.

The Limestone Link is a 36 mile footpath running from Cold Ashton in Gloucestershire to Shipham on Mendip using part of the Kennet and Avon Canal.

At cottages, leave the Link and go left down the lane passing a line of pretty cottages and reach the road in Compton Martin.

4   COMPTON MARTIN

This village's wealth sprang from the paper industry. There were two mills on the stream, which appear to have closed in 1839. The pretty village pond is the source of the River Yeo, the main supply of Blagdon Lake and of a large quantity of water for Bristol. The village is noted for its glorious Norman church, with a fine nave and exceptional vaulting in the chancel. But its other claim to fame is that it was the birthplace of one of our saints, St Wulfric who later lived in a cell at Hazelbury Plucknett, near Crewkerne in Somerset.

Turn left and come to the Ring O' Bells, an award-winning pub with a beautiful garden below the wooded slopes of Mendip.
Retrace your steps along the road and back up the lane to where you came out of the woodland track earlier. Now keep straight on climbing up a

fairly wide track, quite steeply at first. The track bends its way up through the woods, past an old quarry and becomes less steep. This is a very green and beautiful route passing moss covered boulders and ferns.

Near the top there is a choice of paths and here we join the shorter route. Keep straight on.

✦ Shortly go over a stile. Continue on to buildings at Whitegate Lodge.

5   WHITEGATE LODGE

Go out past the house on the drive and through the gate.

Turn right on the lane, passing alongside more of the Hazel Manor woodland. Follow the lane for over half a mile and go round a corner by Hazel Lodge where the drive to Hazel Manor begins. Follow the lane for nearly another mile to the junction with the B3134 cross Mendip road.

Go straight over and take the path ahead. There are two parallel rights of way and I have chosen the right hand one, partly because it is less wet and muddy. Follow it along, passing a large house, Nordrach.

6   NORDRACH

This is now a private house but has had a variety of uses over the years. In the nineteenth century it provided summer holidays for mentally handicapped youngsters, and later became a TB sanatorium, named Nordrach-on-Mendip, after a successful TB sanatorium in Germany's Black Forest, founded by Dr Otto Walther, and employing a rigid fresh air regime. During the Second World War, Bristol Children's Hospital was evacuated to Nordrach and later, as part of Ham Green Hospital Group, it again catered for TB patients. Closing as a hospital in 1956, it soon reopened for refugees from the Hungarian uprising. It was sold into private ownership in 1958 and was for a while a country club but never developed fully.

As the track bends right, continue straight ahead on a smaller, grassy track. Go ahead through a gate into a field and continue ahead along the left edge under a line of beeches. At the end cross a stile into Nether Wood.

This is an important part of Blackmoor Nature Reserve, cared for by the AONB Service at Charterhouse. The trees are mainly ash and beech with some hawthorn and alder.

Follow this beautiful path under more beeches, part of the old drive to and from Nordrach. Ignore a track right and continue on passing on the right at the end the remains of the horizontal flues used in the re-smelting of the lead.

The old slag was heated in the furnace and some lead collected and the the fumes, still lead-laden were then drawn along these flues en route for a tall chimney, leaving deposits of lead on the flue walls. At regular intervals some of the tunnels were closed off and agile small people, maybe children were sent along the flues to chip the lead off the walls, regardless of the danger to their health from the poisonous lead.

Just before the crossing track, you see on your left the crumbling ruins of an old building.

This was Nether Wood Cottage, connected to the lead-reprocessing and maybe used as an office.

At the junction of paths, turn left. Soon pass the footpath you took earlier and continue ahead, retracing your steps along the track back to the start.

When you drive or walk back up the lane to Charterhouse Centre, over in the field on the right next to the copse is the site of an old Roman fortlet and set into the dry-stone wall on your right as you go back up, near the centre, is a pickaxe stone. This is part of a series of stones set into Mendip walls along the National Cycle Route to Cornwall.

If you want to know more about the area, go into the centre where there is an exhibition and leaflets and someone should be able to help.

* *For bus information telephone in office hours, the Chew Valley Bus Project 01225 477609, or after hours and weekends Traveline 0870 6082608)*

❧ The Ring O' Bells, Compton Martin, tel: 01761 221284.

A Choice Piece of Cheddar

Choice 1: Cheddar Head – Bradley Cross – Cheddar – North Side of Gorge – Cheddar Head.

Distance: 7.5 miles.
Duration: Four and a half hours walking.
Map: OS Explorer Map 141. Cheddar Gorge and Mendip Hills West. Reference: 494 532.

Choice 2: Cheddar Head – Cheddar, using the Mendip Explorer Bus.

Distance: 3 miles.
Duration: One and a half hours walking.
Map: OS Explorer Map 141. Cheddar Gorge and Mendip Hills West. Reference: 494 532.

The views on Mendip around Cheddar really are gorgeous as long as the renowned Mendip mist hasn't shrouded everything, so choose a clear day. There's a challenging circular walk and an easy linear version which has no steep sections. If you do the full walk you not only enjoy vistas over the Levels and way beyond, but also spectacular views of the Gorge itself. The circle takes in three quite different Somerset Trust Nature Reserves and their information boards give an indication of the flora and fauna you are likely to enjoy. Apart from birds above you may look up to see the occasional quiet glider catching the thermals, out from the gliding club on the southern ridge along this part of Mendip. There are plenty of places to get refreshment in Cheddar.

Choice 1 This is only If you are fit, enjoy tackling several steep uphill and some downhill sections and have several hours. An old Mendip drove takes you gently to the southern edge of the Mendips with great views south over the Levels, and then down the West Mendip Way to Cheddar village and Gorge, passing a late Saxon villa. See some of the pretty cottages in the back of Cheddar and complete the circle in spectacular style by walking along

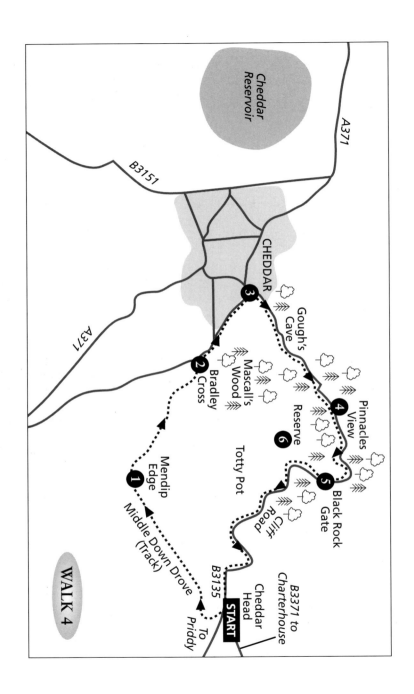

WALK 4

Cheddar Reservoir

A371

B3151

A371

CHEDDAR

3

Gough's Cave

2 Bradley Cross

Mascall's Wood

Pinnacles View

4

Reserve

6

Totty Pot

5 Black Rock Gate

Mendip Edge

1

Cliff Road

Middle Down Drove (Track)

B3135

Cheddar Head

B3371 to Charterhouse

START

To Priddy

the northern edge of the Gorge with an unparalleled view of it. The second half is a challenge with a lot of uphill walking – a couple of them steep, but take your time and it's worthwhile. Allow plenty of time for the walk, views, and Cheddar village with refreshment, the Gorge, Caves and other visitor attractions.

Choice 2 This is the first half of the walk down into Cheddar to catch the Chew Valley Explorer bus back (either to the car at Cheddar Head or all the way back to Bristol). Running on Sundays or Bank Holidays until the autumn from Bristol to Cheddar (First Badgerline 673 and 674), it is a new venture to encourage people to visit the Mendips without cars. (See the end for details.)

Dogs can enjoy either option, provided they are kept under control near farm animals and depending on what you plan in Cheddar. They are welcome on the bus.

Go to Cheddar Head. This is up the top of the Gorge on the B3135 just opposite the turn to Charterhouse and Compton Martin, B3371. There are a couple of lay-bys there, and the bus will stop here if asked.

START

From the lay-by opposite the Compton Martin turn, go through the gate onto the marked path – Middle Down Drove – which is a good broad track. Gently climb uphill, passing a substantial dew pond for animals on the right. Go through a gate and carry on.

Soon pass the first of the Nature Reserves, the 100 acre Middle Down Drove. Before long a sweeping view unfolds south across to Nyland Hill (looking like a balding cleric) the Somerset Levels, Polden Ridge and west to Wales.

1 MENDIP EDGE

Near the edge of the escarpment go through a gate and turn right on the West Mendip Way, heading towards Cheddar and Cheddar Reservoir down below. Start to descend. Go through a gate and keep on down. Pass farm buildings on the left and just continue straight on, through a metal gate and onto a sunken track. It is stony and quite difficult underfoot so go carefully.

After about five minutes, at a large oak tree on the left of the path, you may be able to see over in the field on the left the site of a villa which has been excavated by a team from Bristol University. Probably, late Saxon, it was one of several agricultural dwellings spread along this very ancient route, forming the hamlet of Carscliff. There was still evidence of dwellings right up to the nineteenth century.

On the West Mendip Way looking across to Cheddar Reservoir and Mendips.

Reach a gate and in the field follow the grassy track down and ahead. Half way down, ignore the rather confusing West Mendip Way marker which seems to suggest you bear right. Just continue on the track which curves round and drops down to a gate. Follow a well defined track all the way down to cottages at Bradley Cross and a t-junction of tracks.

2 BRADLEY CROSS

Turn right immediately along a track which begins to climb. Keep on following the West Mendip Way signs in the Cheddar direction. Go through a gate by cottages and carry on to reach a junction by sheds. Turn right on a grassy path and shortly, just before woods (Mascalls Woods in the care of Somerset Wildlife Trust), turn left. Depending on the season, it may be a little overgrown along here for a short way. Follow it for about quarter of a mile. Just before a gate, look to the right to see the crumbling remains of one of Mendip's old lime kilns used for burning lime to spread on the fields. The path carries on, going through another gate, and to a t-junction of tracks.

Turn left on a wide track all the way to cottages on the edge of Cheddar. Turn left and just past the first cottage, go right on a small path which drops down steps to a lane. Turn right down to the village.

3 CHEDDAR VILLAGE

For the bus, turn left across a bridge and, opposite the Riverside Inn is Tweentown, a right turn to Weston-super-Mare. The bus stop is up on the right.

The village of Cheddar was an important Roman and Saxon centre with its wealth based on farming and cheese making for which it was famous as early as 1170 AD. In the seventeenth and eighteenth centuries, the many watermills ground corn and made paper, and, from the Victorian period there was large scale production of clothing. Tourists started to come in significant numbers after the opening of Cheddar Valley Railway in 1869/1870, which provided workers from towns with the opportunity to enjoy a day's outing for the first-time as a Bank Holiday. Gough's Cave is an internationally famous archaeo-logical site because of its Late Upper Paleolithic finds (12-13,000 years old) and contained Britain's oldest complete skeleton (9000 years old). It lies within an Area of Outstanding Natural Beauty and is a candidate for Special Area for Conservation status.

For the full walk: Turn left across the bridge and then take the right turn before Tweentown by the side of the fish and chip shop and go uphill. There's soon a good view over Cheddar village and across to the Gorge. Bend left on the lane past pretty cottages and then right up Tutters Hill. Climb fairly gently and bend left. Just past a cottage, turn right up a steep made-up drive/track (if you get to Rockland House you have gone too far). After a couple of minutes, fork left on the upper path which is the Gorge Walk and now brace yourself for quite a steep ascent.
Go through a kissing gate, and left and continue on up eventually reaching a waymark stile. Cross and turn sharp right immediately. Follow the path to the edge of the gorge where a dry stone wall was being repaired when I came here – a never ending task on Mendip. Turn left keeping the wall and Gorge over on your right and still climbing through a meadow which is full of wildflowers in Spring and Summer. Reach a waymark post and for the full view of the Pinnacles and Gorge go right.

The Gorge is the largest in Britain and the Gorge Cliffs are the country's highest inland limestone cliffs. The Gorge is a Site of Special Scientific Interest because of the calcareous grassland, Karst limestone buttresses and horseshoe bats.

4 PINNACLES VIEW

Cross a stile with a National Trust Caution sign. It's a few minutes steep walk down steps to a rocky ledge where the views are breath-taking but it's not for those with vertigo. There are great opportunities for bird watching, particularly to see the peregrine falcons that nest in the cliff. Keep children and dogs well under control.
Return to the waymark post and continue up with the Gorge on your right.

Anywhere in the Gorge area you may see some of the soay sheep which keep the scrub in check.

Go through a wooden gate – another good viewpoint – and continue along the edge of the Gorge all the way, until the path takes you steeply down many steps – 131, I am told.
At the bottom go straight ahead and over a stone slab stile in the wall ahead. Cross the rough field and continue on the path through bracken and then through a wooded area. Cross a stile and go through woodland – here the path is not always very obvious. You drop down to a stony track at the bottom and turn right over the stile, entering Black Rock Nature Reserve.

This is an area of rough grassland, plantation, natural woodland and scree and is an internationally recognised dormouse site. Over 200 species of wild flowers and trees have been identified in the Reserve.

Soon reach Black Rock Gate.

5 BLACK ROCK GATE
Cross straight over the road and climb up steeply through woodland on this rocky path. At the top go through a gate and continue on; shortly keep your eyes open for the West Mendip Way which forks left towards Draycott. The sign is sometimes rather hidden in the trees.
After about 230 metres at a junction of paths go ahead across to a marked stile hidden up in the corner. Keep on, bearing slightly away from the stone wall on a grassy path which leads you down through gorse bushes – a wonderful sight when in bloom. Again, you are back with the Somerset Levels views.

6 RESERVE
Cross a stile ahead into Bubwith Acres Nature Reserve and drop downhill. Just before a gate and another Reserve information board, turn sharp left back on yourself going gently uphill. Follow the path through a gate and continue on along the edge of the hill for about ⅓ of a mile. The path leads up to a waymark stile where you exit the Reserve.
Bear up right on the path through a rough open area. Over on the right are rocks and an old lime kiln. Keep on up and across to the far wall and a gate with waymark sign. Head across the next field to the middle of the left side, passing a lone ash tree on your left and a shed and pond on the right. Cross a double stile, go across the field, and over another double stile. Head up

across rougher ground and then bear right to a gate/barrier – a very rickety affair. (In this area, not far away on the left is a lae mesolithic burial site at Totty Pot being investigated by Bristol University.)

Go ahead bearing slightly away from the right wall to a track and follow it to the right downhill. At the left hand bend before the road, leave the track and go straight ahead in the same direction as before. Resist the temptation to take a path going up right. The path stays just above the first ridge. Cross a crumbling wall. Keep on along the path through bracken and scrub, paralleling the road. After a few minutes reach a more open area where you can see the road down ahead. Continue on and drop down to the gate and come on to the road. Turn right for about five minutes to Cheddar Head.

BUS: *The Chew Valley Explorer runs at roughly two-hourly intervals, calling at Bedminster and villages in the Chew Valley; the bus then goes up Burrington Combe to Charterhouse and Cheddar (total journey one hour seventeen mins). Get off at Cheddar Head and follow the walk to Cheddar village (about one and a half hours). Catch the bus back from Tween Town in Cheddar village near the Butchers Arms. Ring 0870 608 2608 for details of times.*

Looping the Lake

Ubley – West Town – Blagdon – Ubley

Distance: 5.75 miles.
Duration: Approx three hours walking.
Map: OS Explorer Map 141. Cheddar Gorge and Mendip Hills West.
Reference: 527 583

Blagdon Lake is set in the rolling green countryside of North Somerset below the Mendip escarpment, but still in the Area of Outstanding Natural Beauty. It is beautiful, recreational and functional, being a great walking and lazing spot, a favourite haunt of trout fisherman and bird watchers and also a main supply of the water for the City of Bristol. It is around this beautiful man-made lake that our walk circles, sometimes two or three fields away, and sometimes right along the edge, but for most of the time the lake is in view. There is time to admire the glorious setting and look out for a wide variety of bird life that is attracted here. The stretch along the very edge of the lake is sheltered and south facing, a superb warm picnic or relaxing spot when the sun shines. There is no very strenuous uphill walking although there are a fair few stiles and foot-bridges to cross. Unless you go after heavy rain, it should be reasonably mud free. Wear good boots as usual. We make our way round via a mixture of footpaths through fields, quiet lanes and stony tracks and call in at Blagdon village for a pub lunch. Then it's an easy forty minute walk downhill back to Ubley.

The circle begins in the small village of Ubley, lying to the east of Blagdon, just to the north of the A368 Weston-super-Mare to Bath Road.

At the west end of the Ubley is the village hall. Park in the spacious car park or, if it is full, find somewhere else suitable to leave the car.

START
Turn left from the hall. I have chosen a route that goes through the village

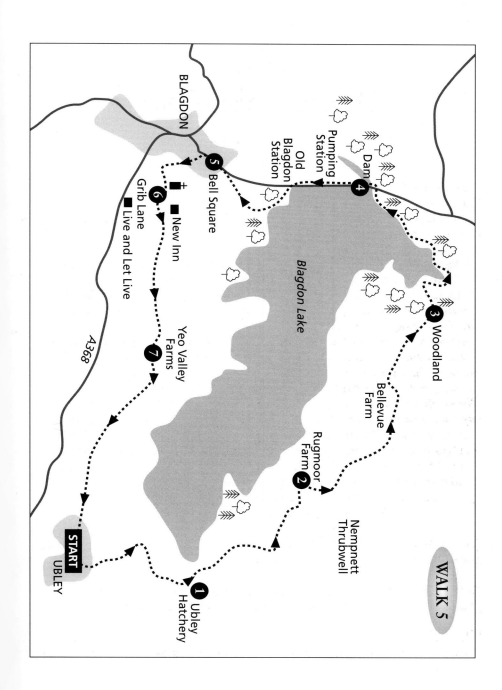

WALK 5

BLAGDON

Pumping
Station

Old
Blagdon
Station

Dam

4

Blagdon Lake

5 Bell Square

New Inn

6 Grib Lane

Live and Let Live

Yeo Valley
Farms

7

A368

START
UBLEY

1 Ubley
Hatchery

2 Rugmoor
Farm

Nempnett
Thrubwell

Bellevue
Farm

3 Woodland

so we can admire some of the old stone houses and church. Pass the tiny village school and then reach the small church of St Bartholomew on the right.

Made of red sandstone, this medieval church has an unusually low tower for this part of Somerset. The absence of pews helps to give a welcome feeling of space. Come out of the church, cross over by the old stone cross and go down Snatch Lane.

On the bend, turn left through a wooden gate on the marked footpath and aim diagonally right across the field, getting your first glimpses of Blagdon Lake. Cross the stile in the centre of the hedge line and continue on in the same direction as before towards the hills down the centre of the field. Cross a stile and go along the right hedge, over a stile/footbridge and ahead in the field to the far left corner. Go through and along a short track to a lane.

Turn left and follow the lane past a stone and brick chimney part of the former mill – it stands in the grounds of the old Mill House.

1   UBLEY HATCHERY
Pass the entrance to the Hatchery.

This is where Bristol Water rears trout for the profitable fishing on Blagdon Lake. Look through the gate at the nutfeeder which attracts nuthatch and great spotted woodpeckers.

Take the lane left towards Nempnett and Butcombe.

The intriguingly named Nempnett Thrubwell is one of the hardest hamlets to find as it is so spread out. It was immortalised in song by The Wurzels 'Down in Nempnett Thrubwell' on the 1976 album 'Combine Harvester'.

You are now enjoying a different and clearer view of Blagdon Lake and of Blagdon village nestling on the north side of the Mendip Hills.

Shortly along here, look for a metal gate on the right and an inventive use of an old army tin hat which has been turned into a snail and sits on the gate.

Just past this house, go over the marked stile on the right. Head across the field to the left of a telegraph pole. Up on the right is an attractive stone house below Breach Hill. Cross a footbridge and two stiles and go up the field with the hedge on your right. Again cross footbridge and stiles and in the next field, turn left along the bottom hedge and go through a marked gate into another field and ahead in the same direction. Cross a stile and plank bridge and head across to the farmyard, aiming just to the right of it, where you cross a stile.

2 RUGMOOR FARM

Go straight over the access concrete drive for the farm and through the marked gate opposite to follow the arrows round the right side of the buildings. Before you reach the corner, go left through a wooden gate and then follow the arrow right and take the farm drive out to the lane.

Turn right and start a gentle climb. Ignore Awkward Hill and just follow the lane to the left and then go right up Chapel Hill. Almost immediately go up stone steps and over a stile. Head up the field, climbing gently, with a beautiful view of the lake and Blagdon village. Cross a stile in the top left corner and turn left on the lane.

The lane takes you along and down to Bellevue Farm. Turn left down the no through lane and once past the farm house, take the marked footpath over a high stone stile on the right.

Go ahead across the field passing to the left of two power poles and cross a stile. Now just continue on in the same direction through three more fields and over stiles with a small stream on your right.

3 WOODLAND

The last stile drops you into woodland onto a stony, dry track – thanks to Bristol Water for the work on this path which not so long ago was a mud bath. When you reach another footpath arrow, note a small path bearing left.

This leads into a sunny open wild flower meadow which gives an unsurpassed view of lake and village and Mendip behind. This area is a favourite haunt of heron and swans and is a wonderful picnic spot. It is certainly worth this small detour. You will probably see fishermen out in boats or casting from the banks.

Return to the path and turn left. Cross a footbridge. Go left over a stile and through woodland. (This is an alternative to going straight ahead over a stile into the field which can be very muddy, and I think this way is prettier.) The path leads to a stile/ barrier by another footbridge. Cross the barrier and turn left over the footbridge. Climb left over another stile and follow the path which winds its way along the edge of the lake, and offers one or two well placed seats in the sun to enjoy the view and look for water birds.

There has been a long tradition of wildfowl counting at the reservoir (dating back to the 1940s) and Blagdon has provided many local birders with their first glimpses of some of the rarer species. There was great excitement when the first pied-billed grebe seen in the Western Palearctic was spotted at the lake in 1963 (and later chosen as the emblem of the Bristol Ornithological Club. When it comes to bird numbers, Blagdon Lake is somewhat overshadowed by neighbouring Chew Valley Lake, twice the size, but suffers far less from disturbance and has more attractive surroundings. There are reedbeds and, when water levels are low, exposed mud that attract passage birds. Wintering waterfowl are the main attraction for birders and the species include most of those seen at Chew Valley Lake. This site has more wintering Ruddy Duck than virtually any other water in Britain and other scarcer species regularly seen here include Goosander, Smew and Bewick's Swan. Great Crested and Little Grebes are present all year but other grebes and divers are rare autumn and winter visitors. Lesser Spotted Woodpecker has been recorded in alders around the lakeshore in winter and passerines at this season can include Stonechat and Grey Wagtail close to the lake, Redpoll and Siskin in the woodlands and Redwing and Fieldfare are often numerous on the farmland.

Breeding birds on the lake are few but Mallard, Gadwall and Tufted Duck nest in small numbers as well as Great Crested and Little Grebes, Moorhen and Coot. The woodlands can be more productive than the lake in summer and hold a good range of the commoner woodland birds. Sparrowhawk breeds in the woods and Buzzard is often seen wandering over the area.

When water levels are low the muddy areas often attract passage waders with Greenshank and Spotted Redshank, Green and Common Sandpipers, and Ruff all regular. Scarcer species such as Little Stint and Curlew Sandpiper are recorded most years. Small numbers of terns pass through the area including regular Black.

Rare waders have included Long-billed Dowitcher, Buff-breasted and Pectoral Sandpipers from North America and Marsh Sandpiper from the east. The North American Ring-necked Duck has also been recorded.

Across the lake set in front of pine trees is the picturesque black and white timbered fishing lodge.

4 DAM
Come out by a stone bridge and overflow by the dam.

North side of Blagdon along the path.

It was built at the end of the nineteenth century. Blagdon Lake, originally called the Yeo Reservoir, was formed in order to tap more of the water sources of Mendip for the rapidly growing urban population of Bristol. A 700 yard long earth embankment was made across the shallow valley to dam the River Yeo and 450 acres of farmland were flooded. The dam was built in eight years amost entirely by hand with much labour coming from all parts of England and Scotland. Water from springs at Rickford are also piped to the reservoir. The lake holds 1700 million gallons of water. To ensure water purity, the village of Butcombe, Compton Martin and Blagdon were provided with good sewage disposal facilities as were neighbouring farms. Bristol Water planted conifers, often alongside tributary streams, so that the roots would prevent scouring during heavy rains in order to reduce the amount of silt deposited into the lake. Surprisigly, the average depth of the lake is only about 14 feet.

Cross a stile at the end of the lake path and come onto the lane.

Turn left on the lane over the dam towards Blagdon up on the hill. It's worth crossing over to see the grounds of Blagdon's Victorian Pumping Station, which you soon pass over on the right.

This impressive red brick building in spacious grounds is also Bristol Water's Visitor Centre. From early in May until mid September it is open to the public every Sunday afternoon from 2-5pm with free entry. Visitors of all ages can enjoy a range of activities and exhibitions. You can see the working Victorian giant beam engine, help to feed the trout, follow the nature trail and look at exhibitions on water and the environment. For details telephone Bristol Water head office in Bristol on 01179665881.

At the end of the dam, turn left on to Park Lane with lake on your left.

However, before doing that if you go straight on a few yards and look to the right you see the old Blagdon station, now a private house. This was on a branch line of the aptly named 'Strawberry Line' (Yatton to Cheddar) – part of Bristol and Exeter Railway. It was famous for transporting the popular strawberries from

Cheddar to markets via Bristol. This little branch was a very picturesque route from Congresbury via Wrington to Blagdon and was finally closed in 1950 a long time before the final closure of the whole branch line which carried on until 1963. A very active Cheddar Valley Railway society has been working hard to establish a footpath and cycle way along the old railway and has a hope that one day it might be possible to bring it along to Blagdon from Wrington.

To continue, go along Park Lane and after a few minutes, turn right up Dark Lane, opposite the entrance to Blagdon fishing lodge. Follow this ivy and fern-bedecked lane with a reasonable hard core underfoot. It is uphill, but well graded and not difficult.

At the top, turn left more steeply up the lane into Blagdon – this is the steepest section of the walk.

5   BELL SQUARE

Turn left into Bell Square which contains some of the oldest cottages in Blagdon and take the footpath out the back which heads across towards the other side of Blagdon and the imposing church with its 116 ft high tower – one of the highest in the country. Follow the path through gates towards the church passing Tim's Well.

This was one of the village's only two water supplies and was restored to mark the Queen's Silver Jubilee in 1977. Carrying full buckets of water from the well up the hill and home must have been a strenuous chore.

Follow the path up to the church – you can go through the churchyard or along the path at the side.

The church is filled with light and colour and the present building dates back to the early part of the twentieth century when it was rebuilt by William Henry Wills of tobacco family fame. He turned an ugly church to one of beauty and he lies in the shadow of the tower, under a granite cross – the first and last Lord Winterstoke. It is said that the two main influences on life in Blagdon have been the Wills family and the lake. The Wills family came to the village as Lords of the Manor bringing the prospect of wealth and employment. Another famous person buried in the churchyard is John Langhorne who was the translator of Plutarch's Lives. He was rector of Blagdon until his death and while working on the translation.

From the church go out along the entrance lane/drive and this brings you to Park Lane with the New Inn opposite.

The pub has glorious views of the lake from the garden and car park. Please note that it is closed on Mondays. If you want an alternative, then turn up Park Lane for about three minutes to the main road at the top and the Live and Let Live pub.

If you do this, you pass Hannah More's House, set up in the closing years of the eighteenth century as a school for poor children by the reformer, Hannah More whose philanthropic work touched several Mendip villages, particularly where there were poor and uneducated mining families.

6   GRIB LANE
To continue, take Grib Lane which is just up from the New Inn, and is sign-posted to the cemetery. From the lane are perhaps the best of all views of the full extent of the lake. Continue ahead on the footpath at the end of the lane. Drop down, ignoring a footpath and stile left. Continue down and then bend left to climb over a stile into a field. Turn right along the top edge of the field. Cross a stile and continue on as before in the field, over another stile. Near the end of this next field go right over a marked stile by an oak tree. Follow the arrow along the left edge of the field. Veer over slightly to the right at the end to a stile on the far side on to a crossing track between farms.

There is a large flock of Canada geese that usually frequents the farmland in this area from July to April.

7   YEO VALLEY FARMS
This is Yeo Valley Farms (of yoghurt fame).

The name Yeo Valley began when an independently owned company was set up in 1974, in Blagdon to produce yoghurts and desserts. In 1994, a few of the neighbouring farmers moved over to organic milk production, gained Soil Association approval and set up a co-operative called OMSCo (Organic Milk Suppliers Co-operative). It is now the UK's leading organic milk marketing organisation with over 350 farmers across the UK, which is the majority of organic milk produced in this country. OMSCo represents approximately 85% of the total UK organic milk production and has more dairy farms in the process of converting to organic production.
Organic yoghurt was first made at Yeo Valley's production plant in 1993, when these founder members of OMSCo were looking for a ready market for their milk. Although the level of consumer demand for organic dairy products was low at

that time, Yeo Valley saw this as an opportunity to benefit from a local supply of organic raw material. In 1996, the company set up a second business called The Yeo Valley Organic Company Ltd, solely to produce organic products. The company has two organic production sites employing around 200 people – Cannington in Somerset and Heathfield in Devon.

Cross straight over and go through a small plantation of trees. Cross another concrete path and follow the arrow ahead through a car park. Go into the field and head down the line of power poles to a stile in the corner. Cross two stiles here and in the next field, head across, bearing a little to the right. Go over another marked stile and in this field keep straight on along the left hedge and then veer a little away to the right to a stile in the far hedge. Once over this, walk to the far right corner, through the gate and follow the track which goes to the left side of farm buildings and farmhouse. Come into a lane (Frog Lane) and continue on, shortly reaching the village hall and Ubley.

New Inn, Blagdon, tel: 01761 462475.
Live and Let Live, tel: 01761 462403.

WALK 6

Fair Priddy

Priddy – Deer Leap – Durston Drove – Priddy

Distance: About 5.5 miles.
Duration: Approx two and a half hours walking.
Map: OS Explorer Map 141.   Cheddar Gorge and Mendip Hills West.
Reference: 528 509

Starting on the green in the highest village on Mendip, Priddy, we walk to the unrivalled viewpoint of Deer Leap through an open access area with the remains of a medieval settlement and gaze out over the vast expanses of the Somerset Levels. Then using one of the old droves make our way back, get a good view of Priddy Nine Barrows and past Priddy church before reaching the green again. You can start and end at Priddy Green where the New Inn or the Queen Victoria are very welcoming, or alternatively start at Deer Leap viewpoint and car park and circle round to Priddy for refreshment at the centre of the circle. The going is virtually flat and could be sunny along the southern slopes, but you are also exposed to the prevailing, bracing winds so wrap up well.
Obviously, after heavy rain the footpaths are likely to be wet underfoot. It is splendid all year round and in season there will be a wide range of limestone grassland wild flowers, butterflies and many different birds.

You can start in Priddy village 800ft up in the heart of Mendip and park on the green in the centre near the New Inn. Priddy is north of Wells and can be approached from various directions, and by and large is well signposted.

Or, if starting at Deer Leap: *from Priddy pass the New Inn on your right and then the Queen Victoria and keep on for about a mile and a quarter on the lane leading to Ebbor Gorge, Wookey Hole and Wells. On the right you will see Deer Leap picnic area and car park. Follow the walk from **

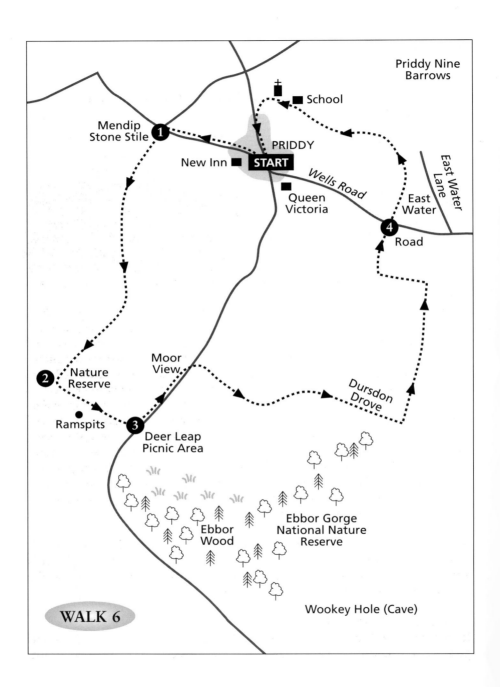

Priddy Nine Barrows

School

Mendip Stone Stile ①

PRIDDY

New Inn ■ START

Wells Road

East Water Lane

Queen Victoria

East Water

④ Road

② Nature Reserve

Moor View

Dursdon Drove

Ramspits

③ Deer Leap Picnic Area

Ebbor Wood

Ebbor Gorge National Nature Reserve

Wookey Hole (Cave)

WALK 6

50

If starting at Priddy:

START

Priddy Green. Walk down the side of the green away from the New Inn, with the green on your right.

Priddy, whose name comes from Prid, a Celt word meaning high, is now a prosperous village with a real sense of community – but its history is rooted in sheep farming, wool production and lead mining. You can't fail to notice on the green the restored thatched hurdle stack, a much photographed reminder of the 600-year-old annual Sheep Fair held on the Green at the end of August. The Fair was origi-

Hurdle stack on Priddy village green.

nally held at Wells, but had to be brought up to the healthier high air of Priddy to escape the ravages of the Black Death and continued in this Mendip village since then, except for the year of the Foot and Mouth outbreak when all country activities including the Fair were halted. It was set up as a mart for the enormous amount of wool produced on Mendip and the woollen cloth and products made by cottagers, spinning and weaving. During the eighteenth and nineteenth centuries, the Fair was also a place where the lead miners working in the mines just outside the village could buy working clothes and boots. Still today it attracts horse traders and sheep farmers and has a wide variety of market stalls. It has the distinction of being the first place where traders used unified measures. Tradition has it that the first rain after Priddy Fair is the beginning of winter, according to Robin Atthill in the book Mendip a New Study. Nowadays another annual event for which the village is becoming famous is the Folk Festival over a summer weekend featuring leading folk artistes.

At the end of the Green continue up the lane marked to Draycott, which rises gently. Continue with good views across the farmland and fields around Priddy. Opposite a lane coming in on the right, turn left on the marked public footpath over a Mendip stone stile by a gate.

1 MENDIP STONE STILE

Ignore the West Mendip Way which forks off right in the field and instead go straight ahead up the left wall of the field on a different public footpath.

In the corner cross a marked stile and continue up the left wall a short distance to another stone stile. Cross and carry on as before following the left wall all the way to the corner. Cross the stile and again follow the wall on your left. You are heading for the southern escarpment of Mendip. In the corner of the next field, cross a wooden stile and immediately a stone stile.

Once over, head straight across the field, in the same direction as before. (If you bear over to the left a little you will join another path which has come in from the left.) Go over a marked stone stile in the far wall and head across the next field, and cross another marked stile.

Now, keeping on as before, following the left wall and soon superb views of the Somerset Levels will unfold below. Over on the left is an area of open access land. Follow the wall until you come to a stile ahead and an information board.

2 NATURE RESERVE

The information board is about Cook's Field Nature Reserve below in which you are free to wander.

But to continue our circle, turn left at this point over a stone stile and head across the open access area with the Levels below on the right and again enjoying a widespread panorama. If the sun is shining, you should get the best of it here on this south facing edge.

Down on the right as you head across you will see a small restored barn, post medieval which was restored by Somerset County Council. These are the most visible remains of a medieval settlement, Ramspits, which consisted of two dwellings, barns, enclosures, ponds. You can explore the area if you wish and will see remains of old walls and tracks but without a guide your imagination will have to do the work. Educational groups who come to Ramspits are able to use the barn as a temporary shelter/centre for their field studies. Look out for buzzards and kestrels which are frequently catching the thermals and hunting along this southern Mendip edge.

To continue, keep more or less parallel with the wall over on your left and when your grassy path forks, stay on the upper path and continue ahead, going through a hunting gate into Deer Leap picnic and parking area.

3 DEER LEAP PICNIC AREA

This is one of the most beautiful viewpoints on the Mendip plateau giving an unrivalled panorama across the Somerset Levels.

* From Deep Leap car park, turn left up the lane. This runs from Priddy down to Ebbor Gorge and Wookey Hole. After less than ½ mile, pass Moor View cottage on the left, and shortly afterwards turn right on a stony track which is Dursdon Drove one of the old tracks used to move animals across Mendip.

Pass a bungalow and farm and when the track comes to a gate and field, turn left on the track which is narrower for a while and less dry underfoot. After rain there may be some mud here, but not for long. Follow the path gently down and then it rises and meets a wider, stony track. Continue ahead on this, ignoring a path going left to Priddy which only returns you to the road. Reach a farm drive going left over a cattle grid and take this.

Follow this good dry flat track and follow it as it bends left. Cross another cattle grid and turn right. Here as you look ahead you should get a good view of some of the Priddy Nine Barrows on the horizon.

These Bronze Age burial mounds and the adjoining Ashen Hill barrows are ancient landmarks of this part of Mendip.

Pass a farm and reach a road.

4 ROAD

Cross over and go over the stile opposite following the marked footpath to Priddy church and Eastwater Lane. Go up the field following the left wall and going gently uphill. Cross a stile and go ahead across a small field and up and over a ladder stile.

Eastwater is a centre for two caving clubs with another popular swallet here to give access to the caving system. A swallet, or sink hole, is a vertical entry cave.

Fork left and go down the field, to the end and over another ladder stile in the wall and continue on in the same direction keeping fairly close to the wall on the left. Ahead you will start to see Priddy church and its stocky thirteenth century grey tower.

At the far end of the field go left through a gate opening marked with a yellow footpath arrow. Now head down the field fairly close to the right wall. Cross a super Mendip stile with steps at the end. Head straight across the field in the direction of Priddy church, dropping down into a dip. There cross a stone stile ahead, followed immediately by a wooden stile. You need to head up to the top left corner of this field, and a good way is to go left immediately along the bottom of the field and when you reach the corner, turn right uphill with the wall on the left. At the top ahead of you a yard or two from the top left corner is a stone stile. Cross and go between Priddy hall and primary school and turn right to a small green.

It is worth visiting the church, which is much prettier inside than it may look. The modern stained glass window showing a girl and a pony is of interest and was installed in memory of Catherine Gibbons, from Eastwater Farm who died after a long illness. The church contains a primitive font, a simple screen, stone pulpit and a tablet which records 'this tower was mended and two pinikls 1705'. The churchyard is well tended and very much in keeping with the surrounds. In spring you may see primroses, a rarity in such a high place.

Go left down a tarmac lane across the green to a road on the edge of Priddy. Turn left back to the main village green.
If you are half way through the circle, go down the right side of the green, passing Manor Farm on your right.

This ancient Priddy farm is also the site of Manor Farm Swallet, a mecca for the many cavers who come to Mendip.

Then turn right up the lane to Draycott and follow the instructions from there. Probably you will visit the New Inn or the Queen Victoria (a little further on from the New Inn) beforehand. If so, follow the instructions from the beginning.

🐾 The New Inn, Priddy, tel: 01749 676465.
🐾 The Queen Victoria, Priddy, tel: 01749 676385.

Ridge to Ridge

East Harptree Woods – Harptree Combe – Prospect Stile – Hinton Blewett – Coley – East Harptree Woods

Distance: 8.25 miles.
Duration: Four hours walking
Map: OS Explorer Map 141.   Cheddar Gorge and Mendip Hills West.
Reference: 558 541.

This ridge to ridge circle will occupy the best part of a day, by the time you have had a picnic or pub lunch. It is a magical walk weaving together the Mendip escarpment and the last lead smelting chimney on Mendip, with the line of hills to the north on which stands Hinton Blewett village. We start on the flat and then drop down atmospheric Harptree Combe where the stream bubbles its way through wild flowers, ferns and mosses, cross the valley and then climb steeply up to the ridge and pause at Prospect Stile one of the best viewpoints in the area looking across to Mendip. Then we visit Hinton Blewett and the welcoming pub before starting the return which does involve quite a lot of uphill work. Choose a clear day so you get the best of the views and if you go after wet weather be prepared for mud and water underfoot.

Find your way to the Forest Enterprise car park at East Harptree Woods. One way to reach it is to go into East Harptree village and take the lane to the left of the clock which climbs steeply out the back of the village up Smitham Hill heading south. After just over a mile from the village reach the car park on the right set in woodland. There is a barrier and Forest Enterprise East Harptree Woods board. Or go to the Castle of Comfort up on Mendip and take the right hand of the two lanes opposite signed to East Harptree. Pass the communications tower and reach the woodland and entrance on left. Go under the barrier and into the parking area. Be careful not to leave valuables in the car.

START
From the parking area turn left along the broad forest track. After about five minutes take the first surfaced path on the right and follow this through

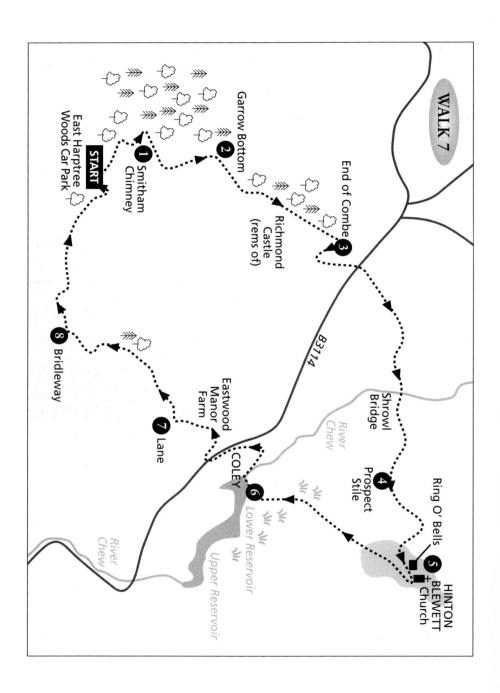

WALK 7

East Harptree
Woods Car Park

START

1 Smitham
Chimney

Garrow Bottom

2

Richmond
Castle
(rems of)

End of Combe

3

B3114

Shrowl
Bridge

River
Chew

4 Prospect
Stile

Ring O' Bells

5 HINTON
BLEWETT
Church

6

COLEY

Lower Reservoir

Upper Reservoir

River
Chew

7 Lane

Eastwood
Manor
Farm

8 Bridleway

woodland – Frances Plantation planted in memory of Countess Waldegrave – until you reach Smitham Pond with the 70ft high stone and brick chimney on the other side. Go along the left side of the pond where a rustic sturdy seat made of 200-year-old oak is a pleasant resting spot. Continue on to an information board just before the chimney

1 SMITHAM CHIMNEY

This is the last lead-smelting chimney on Mendip and is a visible reminder of the thousands of years of mining that have taken place on the hills. This Cornish-style chimney was built in the mid nineteenth century when an industry sprang up here and at three other centres on Mendip to resmelt the piles of slag from previous mining.

Go right, passing the chimney on your right, and drop downhill on the track. On the left covered in trees and vegetation are lines of horizontal flues which connected the chimney with the lead smelter.

Some clearance work by volunteers is being done to give passers-by a better idea of the mining set-up here. Near *Down the path to Smitham Chimney.*

the bottom of the track over on the left see the remains of the slag discarded during the smelting process. The furnace was down in this area.

Cross a stile by a hunting gate and go ahead through the farmyard and on down the farm track. Just before you reach the lane, go left on a track past a bungalow and garage. At the end cross a stile and go down the middle of the field to a stile on the far side.

Already, good views across Chew Valley and lake are opening up, and over on the right is the Hinton Blewett ridge – our destination.

Cross the stile and head downhill to the bottom right corner, passing a big hollow on the right in the field.

This is a swallet hole where the ground has collapsed into the rock fault – a typical feature of limestone areas.

Cross the stile into a wood and immediately take a stile on the right and then go down the left side of the field and cross a stile by the metal gate at the bottom. Once on the lane, turn left coming into Garrow Bottom.

2 GARROW BOTTOM

Just before a farm, go right over a marked stile. Go straight across the field, without climbing up, and cross a stile into woodland and Harptree Combe. Now just follow the path and stream down the combe. It may be wet and lower down you will need to criss-cross your way over the stream.

Harptree Combe is a secluded place, full of bluebells in spring, beech and ash and is an SSI (a Site of Special Scientific Interest).

Reach a small crossing path, up on the right on the top is the site of former Richmont Castle. You could climb up and have a look round; there are some crumbling stone work remains, but very little.
Equally when you carry on down the combe to where the water culvert starts and look up to the right you may see some of the remains.

This was the first big house at East Harptree, a Norman building impressively sited on this steep brow. It is sad that such a beautiful spot was once the scene of much conflict and cruelty. It was originally owned by the cruel Azeline de Percheval, known as the Wolf, and his son, equally cruel who was known as the Wolf Cub. It was a useful fortress during the Norman conquest of Somersetshire. In 1138 it was held by Sir William de Harptree for the Empress Matilda against King Stephen who moved to attack it after laying siege to Bristol. It proved almost impregnable but the King eventually managed to capture it through a ruse which lured the defenders out to their deaths. Fortunately, it appears that the king did not destroy the castle. It passed from the de Harptrees (who were later known as the de Gournays) and then down to the Newton family. In the time of Henry VIII it was pulled down by Sir John Newton who left only a small circular tower (long since gone). Sir John used stone from the castle to build a magnicicent home of his own. No-one is quite sure where the house was but it may have been at Proud Cross on the road up Smitham Hill towards Smitham Chimney. Sir John's tomb is in the porch of East Harptree church. Sir John lies beneath a stone canopy with his eight sons and twelve daughters praying before him.

Carry on following what is now a proper water culvert.

This is part of Bristol Water's amazing water supply taking Mendip water from springs at Chewton Mendip the 12 miles to Bristol relying purely on a gravity-fed system – in other words, no pumps.

Steps lead down to a crossing track. Go left continuing down the combe with high stone walls on the right supporting the water pipeline. Go under the pipe and keep on following the path.

Shortly, look to the right and see some of the impressive slabs of conglomerate forming a sheer wall.

3 END OF COMBE

At the end of the combe, cross a stile and follow the arrow right. Go up between hedges and cross a stile ahead. Walk towards East Harptree village and go left through a metal gate (marked). Follow the left hedge and in the next field make for the bottom left corner. Cross the stepped gate onto a road. Turn left and almost immediately go right over a marked stile. Go down the left hedge and cross a stile a short distance from the corner. Watch out for badger activity in this area which had caused a rather lethal foot trap below the stile when I came here! Go ahead still down the left edge of the field. At the narrow bottom of the field take the stile on the right, joining the Limestone Link.

This 36 mile route links the Cotswolds with the Mendip Hills, starting at Cold Ashton in Gloucestershire and ending at Shipham up on Mendip.

Go right over a stone bridge and another stile. Follow the arrow now diagonally left across the field, passing under the line of telegraph wires, ignoring a stile on the left and reaching the far corner by an oak. Cross a stile and turn left along the lane.

After passing cottages in the settlement of Shrow Bridge, cross one bridge and then a stone bridge ('weak bridge') which spans the River Chew.

Just past this, cross a slab stile on the left and then a plank bridge and follow the right hedge. Go over two stiles into another field and head for the bottom left corner. Cross the stile and turn right and make for another stile situated between a large pylon and stone barn. Go over this and across the next field, crossing another stile to come down to the lane.

Turn right and soon see the Limestone Link sign on a step gate on the left. Here beginneth the climb up! Go across to the hedge and follow it on your left, climbing up sharply. Cross a stile and continue on up. Cross another stile and then take the path which bears up left steeply. At the next ridge continue on up in the same direction to the top corner to a well-known viewpoint, Prospect Stile.

4 PROSPECT STILE
Take a rest on the Jubilee Seat and enjoy the far-reaching views.

Thanks to Hinton Blewett Parish Council for this resting place which celebrates the Queen's Golden Jubilee.

Turn left on a footpath (Spring Lane) between hedges.

This path which used to be a watery, muddy mess has been vastly improved by the parish council and the hedge laid with the help of Mendip AONB Service and students from Radstock College.

At the end, reach a crossing track and go right on the track, or take the footpath which runs parallel just to the right through fields but ends up at the same place – at a junction.
Go left on the lane and follow it as it bends left and goes along past houses to the church.

5 HINTON BLEWETT CHURCH
The present perpendicular style building is of blue lias with and arcade of stone from Doulting quarry near Wells. It dates from the fourteenth century with very sympathetic and expensive restoration work in the nineteenth century which amongst other improvements revealed the beautiful waggon roof. There is an uplifing feeling of light and airiness in the church. The Norman Font is the oldest relic with delicate work and graceful proportions. The lead is original and marks can be seen of the staples by which it was locked against the power of evil spirits! The fifthteenth-century carved bench ends are also of great interest. The tower was rebuilt early in the eighteenth century and the old one was where a quarter of the body of a supporter of the Monmouth Rebellion was hung after being parboiled and dipped in pitch.

Continue on the lane to the Ring O Bells, one of my favourite pubs, nestling behind cottages at the side of the small village green, known as the Barbury.

It was here that copper coins from the reign of the Emperor Claudius were unearthed. On the other side of the road, still on the green, is an oak planted on 14 February 1998 to celebrate the life of Princess Diana.
Hinton Blewett which is well sited on high ground has been a settlement from at least Roman times. Its name derives from Hantune – 'a settlement on high land' and the second name refers to the local landowners, the Bluets, who came here during Edward II reign in the early fourteenth century.

From the pub cross the green, bearing right to the phone box and then follow the Coley/West Harptree road (Lower Road). Continue through the village and turn left into Hook Lane. Take the marked footpath on the right over a stile by a gate and go diagonally left across the field to a stile in the far hedgeline.

Ahead is the Mendip Ridge and Smitham Chimney.

Once over, head across the field to a stile on the far side and go over into another field. Start the descent down Coley Hill going diagonally left, keeping telegraph poles on the right. Cross a stile by a hunting gate and head on downhill in the same direction as before to a large oak. At the side of the oak pick up a grassy track going down, still diagonally left, and in the bottom corner by another oak go ahead to a marked stile. Go right down the field near the right hedge. Cross a stile and come onto the end of the dam for Coley Lower Reservoir.

6 RESERVOIR
This reservoir and an adjoining one were built in the mid nineteenth century by Bristol Water as part of their supply to Bristol and were partly to ensure enough flow of water for the local millers during times of drought. There are no working mills to worry about now, but instead they are used to raise trout for the lakes at Chew and Blagdon.

Cross the dam and then a concrete, iron-railed bridge. Go over a cattle grid and take the track out past the farm to the lane in Coley.
Turn left heading towards Litton and Chewton Mendip and follow it all the way between high-sided banks to the main road. Turn right along the grass verge for a short distance. Cross and take the lane on the left towards Greendown. A couple of yards along, go up steps on the right on the marked footpath and over a stile into a field. Follow the left hedge. Cross a stile by a gate and turn left up the hedgeline. Cross a rather high stile and continue up the hedgeline.

Over to the right is Eastwood Manor Farm which still retains its original Victorian buildings. For many years this was a model farm and was open to the public for farm visits.

Cross a stile in the corner onto a lane.

7 LANE

Turn right and take the first footpath on the left into a field. Go across bearing slightly right towards a gap near the top right corner. Go through and climb up into to another field. Go across and over a stile on the other side. Bear left, heading for the left hand end of the small ridge. Go through a metal kissing gate, well waymarked, and follow the path by the stream. Cross the stream into another field and head up the right hand side of the field with woodland on the right. In the top right corner go into another field and up the fence line. In the corner, with a house over on the right, turn left, still in the field, along the fence line and reach the next corner. Go out through a gate and down to a lane.

Turn right and go uphill along Back Lane. Go round one bend and follow the wall along and at a t-junction, turn right and then right again onto a stony bridleway, Greendown Batch.

8 BRIDLEWAY

Follow this uphill for about five minutes until, near the top, you see a wooden gate on the right, marked with a public footpath arrow. Go up the field parallel with the right hedge. Go through into the next field and continue on along the hill enjoying the panorama across to the north. Cross a stile into the next field and head diagonally left to the top edge. Turn right under a line of beeches and pick up a track going along the top. Follow this along, through a gate. Join a tarmac lane and continue on all the way to a junction with a road. Turn left uphill.

Note the Devon banking on each side – a turf and stone wall topped by a hedge. This is unusual on Mendip and here is due to the former landowner who hailed from Devon.

Turn right into East Harptree Woods and car park.

⮞ Ring O Bells, Hinton Blewett, tel: 01761 452239.

From Cathedral to Combe

Wells – East Horrington – Biddle Combe – Wells

Distance: 7.75 miles.
Duration: Approx four hours walking.
Map: OS Explorer Map 141. Cheddar Gorge and Mendip Hills West.
Reference: 551 459.

About a mile and a quarter of bluebells in a wooded, mossy combe alongside a bubbling brook is a treat during the second half of this interesting Mendip circle near Wells. However, it's great at all times of year and in winter there's the added pleasure of the sun filtering through the bare trees to make the combe lighter. The start is Wells cathedral and we head across The Park before an easy climb up to the Mendip plateau. We visit two Mendip villages, then drop down into enchanting Biddle Combe, past a buddle house and lime kiln, and back to Wells, walking alongside the moat and Bishop's Palace. If you are there at 5pm you can see the swan pulling the bell by the Palace entrance because he wishes to be fed. Much of the going is very easy on dry tracks and lanes but as it is rocky and uneven and can be wet and slippery in the combe, wear good supportive, waterproof boots. There is no refreshment en route so take a picnic and wait until you return to Wells.

Park in Wells and make your way to the Market Square by the Cathedral.

START

Go under the archway at the back of the square to come into the grounds and moat around the Bishops's Palace. Turn right along the tree-lined walk with the moat and crenellated wall of this beautiful Palace on your left. At the end corner of the wall, go straight ahead on to the marked public footpath to Dulcote. This tarmac path has you striding out across the area known as The Park with good views across to Glastonbury Tor

You pass interesting benches designed and made by pupils of the Blue School in Wells. Stay on the path all the way to a lane – about ½ mile distance.

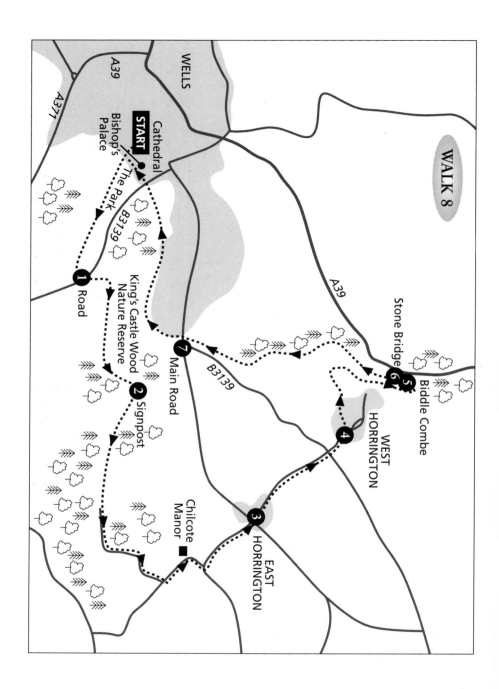

WALK 8

WELLS

A39

A371

START
Cathedral
Bishop's Palace
The Park
B3139

1 Road

King's Castle Wood
Nature Reserve

2 Signpost

7 Main Road

B3139

A39

Stone Bridge 6 5
Biddle Combe

4 WEST HORRINGTON

3 EAST HORRINGTON

Chilcote Manor

Bishop's Palace, Wells.

Come out through a gate and down to a road, the B3139 leading to Dulcote.

1 ROAD

Cross the road and go through the kissing gate and immediately turn left up the field – the only steep uphill section of our circle. There are good views across to Glastonbury Tor and over the Levels as you go. Go over a steep stile and continue up across the next field and over another stile onto a crossing track. Note the brick Second World War pillbox in the field on your left. Turn right, soon going alongside the velvety expanse of Wells Golf Club greens. Stay on the main track all the time and gradually begin to climb very gently.

On your left is the ancient woodland of King's Castle Wood Reserve in the care of Somerset Trust for Nature Conservation leading up to an Iron Age hill fort. If you have time you may like to explore. As the information board points out, there are some interesting flora and fauna to be seen.

When the track forks, stay on the upper, wider track in woodland and start to climb gently. Pass another King's Castle Wood information board and go through a gate and the track climbs more steeply. Reach a junction of footpaths and signpost at the top

You will see that we are following the East Mendip Way which runs from Wells to Cottles Oak near Frome.

2 SIGNPOST

Turn right on the EMW in the direction to Shepton Mallet going across a long field. At the end, a short track leads to a wooden gate. Go through into another field. Continue in the same direction following the left wall and hedge.

At the end go through a hunting gate by a big wooden gate and come onto a track which soon turns into a tarmac lane, Lyatt Lane, which because it is a no through lane, is extremely quiet and ideal for good walking.

In the distance you can see the tall mast of the Pen Hill transmitter, even more clearly than before. After about ½ mile of easy, open walking come to a t-junction with a lane, and turn left. Soon you pass a farm

Look at the low corrugated barn roof on the right which is covered with what looks like a green carpet, but is, in fact, stone crop which should be a picture when in bloom.

Pass Chilcote Manor which has an attached barn which in the fifteenth century was a dwelling. If you come on the hour you will be lucky enough to hear the clear sounds of the Manor's bell ringing out into the Mendip air. Go round the bend and a couple of minutes, take the first turning left. This lane, Chilcote Lane, offers great views across towards Wells. After about ⅓ mile reach the outskirts of East Horrington village.

On the left is an attractive recent addition to the village architecture, the millennium lychgate which leads to the graveyard.

3 EAST HORRINGTON

At the main road, cross over onto the lane opposite heading towards West Horrington. You pass a number of gracious stone houses in East Horrington including the Manor House. It is about ½ mile along to reach another main road, the Bath Road. Cross and continue in the same direction along the no through lane towards West Horrington.

4 WEST HORRINGTON

Pass the village signstone commemorating the Queen's Jubilee. At a bend, just past a farm, go left on the marked footpath along a tarmac/concrete track. Continue on this track which becomes grassy. The village is up on the right. Cross the stile at the end and go along the right hedge. Cross another stile and continue on the track along the top of the wood with Biddle Combe down below. Reach a gate on the right leading to the village and a well positioned seat, with another circular tree seat over on the left. Continue ahead on the track soon starting to descend gently into the combe. After about a third of a mile come down to the combe and the stream and a circular stone building.

5 BIDDLE COMBE

On the right is a restored buddle house, a visible link with the previous lead mining industry in the area. No-one quite knows how the buddle house was used but it was probably part of the washing process for the mined ore.

Cross the plank bridge and go across a few yards and up onto the path above. Turn left, almost going back on yourself with the stream on your left.

This combe is beautiful at all times of the year, most obviously at bluebell time, but in winter it has the added advantage of letting the winter sun down through the bare branches giving more light. The bright green mosses are a wonderful contrast.

6 STONE BRIDGE

When you reach a stone bridge left over the water, and a footpath sign, keep straight on along the path to Wells, still with the stream on the left. The path can be quite heavy going along here, especially where it is narrow, what with the slippery stones, possible mud and water, but it is still a very special and beautiful area. At one point you need to cross over the stream onto the path on the other side, but it should be fairly obvious. Then carry on with the stream on your right. Later on the path takes you back over the stream. You find you are leaving the woodland and coming into an open valley with the stream over on the left. Pass a large lime kiln on the right.
Continue on and eventually you pick up a track which takes you to the main road, via a hunting gate and large metal gate.

7 MAIN ROAD

On the corner on the left is the entrance to the old Mendip Hospital, founded in 1848, now part of a private residential development.

Cross the main road to the right of the City of Wells sign and at the left side of the bus shelter, take the path which is signed as Wells Golf Club. Go along here, with gardens on your right. Bend left with the path with golf course on your left and hedge and stream on right and after about 50 yards go right following the path back on itself on the other side of the small stream. Continue on in the direction you were in before, with sports fields on the left and gardens coming down to the stream on the right.

Ahead you can start to get really good views of the East End of Wells Cathedral. At the end of the sports fields, carry on – the path soon becoming tarmac. Reach a road and cross more-or-less straight over, going through a metal barrier. You come alongside the Bishop's Palace moat again. Turn right at the end and retrace your steps back to the Cathedral and to where you began.

WALK 9

Fort Favourite

Oakhill – Maesbury Hill Fort – Oakhill

Distance: About 8 miles.
Duration: Four hours walking.
Map: OS Explorer Map 142, Shepton Mallet and Mendip Hills East.
Reference: 474 633

Try and go on a clear day with good visibility to enjoy this walk to the full. The East Mendip countryside to the north of Shepton Mallet in Somerset is typical open, pleasant farming land which many walkers may not have discovered. It has an ancient, undisturbed feel about it and has several historical gems – Maesbury Castle, an Iron Age fort which on the right day can give you breathtaking views, the old Roman Road, the Fosse Way, round barrows and a former beacon and boundary stone. The smell of hops and malt at the brewery at the start of the walk may whet your appetite for the pub en route – about two thirds of the way round. There is a reasonably gentle climb up to the Fort (remarkably easy because we are starting high at 600 ft and climbing to 1000 ft) and the rest is easy going on quiet lanes and tracks. This walk is also notable for the bluebells in Beacon Hill Wood.

Go to the East Mendip village of Oakhill (600 ft above sea level) which lies on the A367 north of Shepton Mallet. Find somewhere safe to park – I chose the High Street which leads down off the A367 opposite the Oakhill Inn. If this is not suitable you could park along the Leigh on Mendip road at the side of the Oakhill Inn. (If you do this, to start the walk come to the main road and take Dye Lane opposite which takes you down to the High Street and then turn left – this is the very end of the walk.)

START

Walk along the High Street, passing Zion Hill on the right, a disused part of Oakhill Brewery and then you will start to be aware of the tantalising smell of hops as you reach the present Brewery at the Old Maltings.

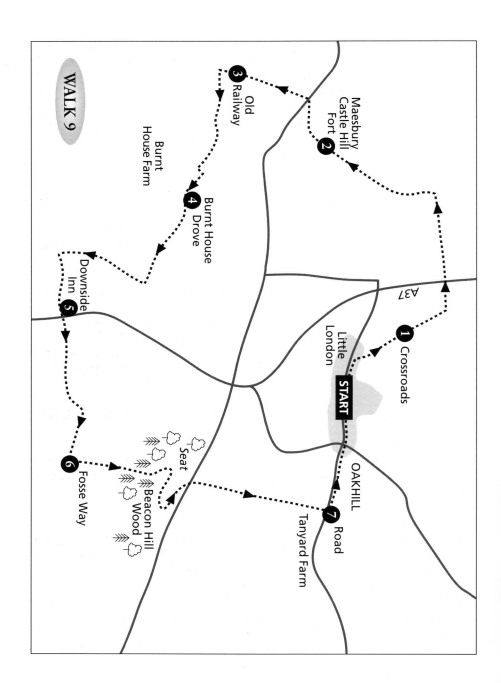

WALK 9

Old Railway ③

Maesbury Castle Hill Fort ②

Burnt House Farm

Burnt House Drove ④

Downside Inn

⑤

A37

Little London

Crossroads ①

START

OAKHILL

Seat

Fosse Way ⑥

Beacon Hill Wood

Tanyard Farm

Road ⑦

70

Brewing has been an important industry in Oakill since Oakhill Brewery was founded by John Billingsley in 1767. It became a huge success, building its own railway line to deliver beers throughout Wales and the West Country. The heyday was before the first World War when over 2000 barrels of stout a week were transported on the brewery railway. Sadly it never recovered from a huge fire in 1925, and was bought by Bristol United Breweries which merely used the remains of the buildings as a depot. In 1981 the microbrewery Beacon was founded in the old fermenting room, but only lasted until 1983. A year later Reg Keevil revived the brewery, first calling it Old Brewery Oakhill, then simply Oakhill, producing five keg beers and six bottled beers. The brewing was moved in 1997 to the the old brewery maltings to allow for expansion. The original brewery company built many of the houses in Oakhill, supplying much of the village with gas, water and sewerage. To the east of Oakhill is a 15ft depression in a field said to be where the brewery horses were buried, along with rubbish.

Opposite a small disused graveyard, reach an area known as Little London.

It seems that on the very old maps, Little London was actually on the other side of the main road. The cottages were originally very basic, built by the miners in twenty four hours which gave them a right of ownership. In order to make their cottage and the area seem much finer than they really were, the mining families frequently chose rather grand names – hence Little London.

Take the right fork which goes up a small hill. After about 200 yards there is a footpath sign on the right.

Although not on the route, it is interesting that in the field here are the remains of a small scale steam railway – run for several years by the Oakhill Manor Railway.

1   CROSSROADS

Continue up the road to a crossroads. Take the marked footpath opposite through a steel gate and into a field. Follow the right hedge ahead through two fields, crossing a stone stile and reaching another stone stile at the end which brings you over onto an ancient drove, Limekiln Lane.
Go left along the drove and follow it to the busy A37. Cross and continue along the drove on the other side. Cross a wooden stile at the end and then continue straight ahead across the field, over a stile and onto Roemead Lane. Turn left and after about 200 yards cross the busy Cheddar road, bear

slightly right to cross another stone stile. Follow a stream on your left and cross another stone stile. There's a crossing path/track here. Go right. Almost immediately cross a small stream, and then bear left following the stream on your left up to and through a farm gate.

Maintaining the hedge on the right, climb fairly gently up through two more fields and over two stiles and then a short stretch of path and over another stile to arrive at what is the outer defensive wall of Maesbury Castle Iron Age fort.

2 MAESBURY CASTLE
Go ahead over this bank and up to the main wall-bank.

From the top of this inner defence, at 1000 ft above sea level, providing the visibility is fair, there are panoramic views in every direction, from the Wiltshire Downs to Exmoor, and from the Welsh mountains to the Dorset Heights and Cranborne Chase. Closer by lies the whole of the East Mendip plateau and surrounding you is a varied landscape of green hills and valleys punctuated with familiar landmarks such as Dundry, Alfred's Tower, Glastonbury Tor and Wells Cathedral. The very name, Maesbury, means hill fort and seemingly it was a very strong one.

Go more or less straight ahead across the centre of the encampment and down into the ditch to reach a stile ahead, just to the right of woodland. Cross over into the field and then go diagonally down across the field to a steel gate below which comes onto a road.

Go right and within about 25 yards, go left on the Croscombe and Dinder road.

3 OLD RAILWAY
After 600 yards the road cuts through a high embankment

At one time this carried the Somerset and Dorset Railway (then known affectionately as the 'Slow and Dirty'). In the days of steam, this line meandered from Bournemouth to Bath (Green Park Station – now a Sainsbury's supermarket), with connections to Bristol via Bitton.

Shortly before a junction on the right, take a rough track to the left, which again cuts through the old railway course. Keep ahead and go through a farm gate and through two fields, with the hedge on your right.

At the far side of the second field, a steel gate leads onto a track which may be little muddy after rain. Follow this track (ignoring a stile ahead) as it makes a number of right angled turns in fairly quick succession and, happily, the surface soon becomes firm. Reach Burnthouse Drove by the entrance to Burnthouse Farm.

4 BURNTHOUSE DROVE
This is one of Mendip's various old routes used initially for moving animals. Continue ahead until the Drove arrives at a t-junction, close by a cottage on the left. Here take the right hand lane and walk downhill towards the old mill, now converted into a dwelling. Pass the mill and cross the bridge, and then climb gently.
Ignore footpath signs until reaching the second road junction on the right. Here go left over a stone stile marked as a footpath. Go up the field following the right hedge, cross a stile and go ahead to a disused farm. Go through a steel gate and ahead through the empty and forlorn farmyard and straight out the other side to pick up a grassy track, the remains of the original drive to the farm.
Cross yet another stone stile to reach the main road (A37).

5 DOWNSIDE INN
Immediately on you left is the Downside Inn, serving a good range of food. After refreshment, cross straight over the busy road and take the marked footpath ahead over a stile. Go along the left hedge, over two stiles and continue on the left hedge as before towards a farm. At the end of the field go left over a marked stile and immediately right over another. Follow the right edge, passing the farm on your right and continuing on to the corner to cross a stone slab stile. Continue straight ahead along the right hedge and over another stone stile. Now, go ahead towards the far side, bearing left under the power lines and cross a stile onto the lane. Turn right and continue along this meandering lane for about 300 yards. Look for a wooden signpost marking the Fosse Way track on the left.

6 FOSSE WAY
This is one of the most famous of the old Roman roads running from Bath to Lincoln and had a fosse or ditch on each side.

Follow this for about ½ mile. The track climbs up towards Beacon Hill Wood – now a Woodland Trust area and famous for its bluebells.

It is an ancient woodland developed over the last 200 years on what was open heathland. The bumpy nature of some of the wood is evidence of past quarrying during the Iron Age and Roman occupation. Immediately after the war, the Foresty Commission deep-ploughed the site and established a mixed plantation and during the 1990s the wood was purchased by the Woodland Trust thanks to the work of volunteers from the Beacon Society, headed by Fraser Townend.

Continue up into the woodland with open land still on the right. Follow the sunken track as it curves left, still climbing up through the woodland. The path then bends to the right and continues up. As you start to near the road a small path goes left to a handsome specially designed seat with great views over the countryside and ancient barrows in the adjacent field so it's worth making a very quick detour and return to this point.

This seat is in memory of Fraser Townend who was largely responsible for establishing the wood.

Immediately opposite this left path, go right on a small track up through the woods. Reach an ancient parish boundary stone, 1766. Go straight ahead behind the stone up on to a bank.

Follow a path and reach an embankment edge. Go left and soon reach a round barrow. Topping this is a standing stone, at the highest point of the wood, marking the site of the old beacon of 1736.

Standing Stone in Beacon Wood.

Remember this area was once open land and the beacon would have linked with Glastonbury Tor's beacon to complete the chain of beacons warning of invasions such as the Spanish Armada.

At the beacon go left down off the barrow and through an opening in a fallen tree and head towards the road, still in the wood. Go left on a track. Before you reach the road, go left again paralleling the road and this comes down to a wooden barrier onto the road. Cross with care.
This is another old Roman road – now a very busy short cut from the A37 to Frome.
Go ahead down the track – the Fosse Way again – as it descends towards Tanyard Farm. After 250 yards notice the boundary stone, marking the two parishes of Shepton and Stoke St Michael, dated 1760.
Ignoring footpath signs to both left and right the track eventually crosses open country. Suddenly, and for no apparent reason, the track takes a sharp left turn and then two right turns to eventually return to the original line of the Fosse Way. Maybe there was once a small Roman fort or defence post here and the path skirted around this area.

7 ROAD
Reach a road and turn left until you reach Oakhill and then the Oakhill Inn on the right. Cross the A367 road into Dye Lane opposite. This narrow old downhill path passes some unusual properties and reaches the village main street, the High Street where you started.

- Downside Inn, tel: 01749 342129.
- Oakhill Inn, tel: 01749 840442, closed lunchtime, Mon. and Tues. at time of writing.

Full Steam Ahead

Doulting – Chesterblade – Cranmore – Chelynch – Doulting

Distance: About 5.5 miles.
Duration: Two and three quarter hours walking.
Map: OS Explorer Map 142.   Shepton Mallet and Mendip Hills East.
Reference: 648 432.

The Somerset countryside to the east of the Bath and West Showground is a network of quiet lanes and footpaths weaving through beautiful combes, woods, and farmland. This ramble has a difference – it calls in at the East Somerset Railway at Cranmore station, a nostalgic reminder of the days of steam. After leaving Cranmore we walk through fields and alongside small quarries – another feature of this part of the world. There's another welcoming pub tucked away in Chelynch and then we follow the East Mendip Way and return to Doulting, visiting a well renowned for its healing and saintly qualities. The going is undulating and easy with no steep hills but after rain the walking through fields is likely to be wet and a little muddy if churned up by animals.

Go to Doulting village which lies on the A361 about 1.5 miles east of Shepton Mallet. In the village, turn north on the road to Chelynch and Shepton Mallet and shortly near a telephone box find the car park alongside a children's play-ground on the left. Or if this looks well used, park safely nearby.

START

From the children's play area, return to the busy A361 road and turn right (in the Shepton Mallet direction). Cross and go down the side of mellow looking Abbey Barn Inn which you may choose to frequent at the end of the circle! Pass two glorious tithe barns dating back to the fourteenth and fifteenth centuries and continue on.

1   RAIL BRIDGE

Cross the bridge over the East Somerset Railway. You never know a steam

76

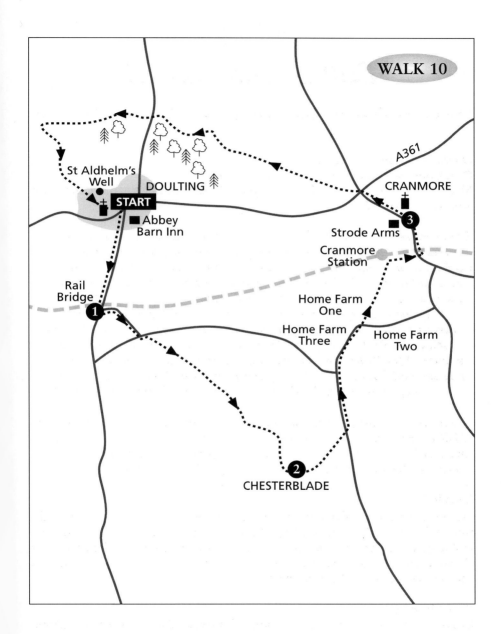

WALK 10

A361

CRANMORE

St Aldhelm's
Well

DOULTING

START

Abbey
Barn Inn

Strode Arms

3

Cranmore
Station

Rail
Bridge

1

Home Farm
One

Home Farm
Three

Home Farm
Two

2

CHESTERBLADE

train may come along just to complete the rural picture! Then turn left towards Chesterblade. Turn left at the next junction and after a few yards, by a gate, go right over a stile marked to Chesterblade. Head diagonally left down the field heading to the left corner of woodland in the middle. Parallel the wood for a short way and then continue on towards the far hedge but veer away left to a hedge corner where there is a gate and foot-path arrow. Go through and down the left edge of the next field. Cross a stile onto a track and over another old stone stile. Head across the field bearing very slightly right to a stile barrier and stile. Go diagonally up the next field heading just to the right of the large pylon. There are pretty views across the tranquil countryside.

Go through into the next field and ahead down the right hedge. At the bottom go right through a marked gate and then left down to the bottom hedge, parallel but a few yards away from the left edge. A metal gate leads to a lane.

Turn right and soon find you are approaching the pretty farming hamlet of Chesterblade.

2   CHESTERBLADE

This hamlet forms one of several tithings within the large parish of Evercreech. (A tithing was originally a Saxon district of 10 householders and later became a distinctive area within the parish assessed for a tithe of land and stock.) By the start of the nineteenth century most of the activity in Chesterblade was concentrated on dairy farming with an emphasis on cheese making. The tiny church, technically a chapelry and not a parish church, is protected by very ancient yews. Inside, St Mary's is very atmospheric and simple, the whitewashed walls contrasting with the colourful beautifully-worked long kneelers made by ladies of the parish. It is interesting that the pews in the eighteenth century were not varnished wood, but painted, often in strong colours. The panels were often white with perhaps blue or dark brown surrounds. As late as 1840, James Allen was paid ten shillings for painting and colouring 'the whole of the interior of the chapel, the pews, pulpit and reading desk'. On the south walls is a poignant memorial to two Chesterblade men who died in the Great War. One of them, Pte Wilfred Carver died at No.29 Clearing Station on Armistice Day itself, 11 November 1918 at the age of twenty one. There is a very detailed history of the church for those who are interested. As you leave, note the very old coffin lid and wooden bier in the porch.

Carry on past the church, ignoring the right turn to Evercreech. Climb uphill through the hamlet and stay on the lane at the top ignoring side turns. After about a third of a mile from Chesterblade, turn right to Cranmore and shortly pass a farm and go round the bend from where you can look across to Cranmore village and church. At the side of Home Farm go left through the gate and hug the side of the farmhouse on your right. (Don't go down the farm drive.) At the end of the garden wall continue on and soon pass a wood on the right. At the end of the wood, go right over two new stiles. Head across the field in the direction of Cranmore church tower. Go through a gate and head across the next field in the same direction and make for the far left corner. Cross a plank bridge, waymarked. Go right with the railway line on your left. Cross another stile and parallel the railway line for a little heading for the far side. Bear away to the right, still heading for the far side, and leave the field through a metal gate onto a lane. Turn left and cross the railway line. Reach the entrance to Cranmore station.

It's worth a visit to see the old style station and booking office, engine shed and rolling stock. There is also a gallery of pictures by the renowned wildlife and railway artist, David Shepherd and East Somerset Models has a wide selection of model railway products. A shop is open most days and the Whistlestop Restaurant is serving when the railway is working. Usefully, there are also toilets.

The rail line opened to Shepton Mallet in November 1858 with an extension to Wells four years later. In 1870 the line reached Yatton through the Cheddar Valley and was known locally as 'The Strawberry Line' as it carried the fruit grown in the Cheddar valley to the fruit markets of London. Cranmore Station closed to passengers in 1963 and to goods three years later. The station would have stayed closed if artist David Shepherd hadn't been looking for a site to house his locomotives and rolling stock displaced by the closure of their site at Longmoor. He built a new loco shed in 1972 and the East Somerset Railway Association was born. The rail enthusiasts' hope is now to extend the line to Shepton Mallet and build a new station.

Go back out to the road and turn left towards the village.

3 CRANMORE VILLAGE

The name of the village comes from Crane Mere, the lake of cranes… But, all I could see when I came where the ducks on the pond opposite the pub!

Turn right and reach the Strode Arms a very welcoming pub in a fifteenth-century former farmhouse overlooking the village duck pond. (Or you can walk on for about another half hour to the quiet country pub at Chelynch.) Continue past the Strode Arms and turn left up Cooks Lane. Then turn left to the church and go round the left side.

This church was also open and I particularly liked the glowing stained glass east window.

Go out the gate on the far side of the churchyard and along a stony path to the road. Turn right. Reach the busy A361 and cross with care and go up the road opposite a yard or two.

Go left over the stone slab stile to the left side of the bus shelter. Make for the far side, a few yards to the left of the small pavilion. The edge of the field was studded with cowslips when I came here. Cross the stile and follow the footpath down the right hedge. Cross a stile ahead, a short way from the far corner, and clearly marked. Go across the centre of the next field and over another stile. Follow the right hedge and at the corner continue on in the same direction, cutting off the right corner. Go through a stone keyhole stile and on through small fields in the same direction with hedge on right. When you reach a field with a cottage up in the far right corner, head up to the cottage diagonally across the field and go through a keyhole stile between cottage and gate.

Go down to the lane alongside the cottage and turn right. Shortly, take the marked footpath on the left. Follow along the left edge, passing alongside two small quarries, where there is still some activity.

Stone (oolitic limestone) has been quarried at various sites around Doulting for hundreds of years and the area provided the stone to build Wells Cathedral. Doulting regularly provides any stone needed for repairs at the Cathedral as the limestone is quite soft.

Continue on, passing along the edge of woodland on your left. Drop down to a stile and go ahead to the side of the cottages to the lane in Chelynch.

4 CHELYNCH

Over on the right is the Poachers' Pocket, another fine Somerset pub. However, our walk continues by going left and then taking the first lane on the right marked to Bodden, which is part of the East Mendip Way.

Together with the West Mendip, this forms a 50-mile-long distance footpath across Mendip.

Ignore the first footpath left, pass a pond on the right and climb gently. At the end of the wood go left over a stile on the marked path. Follow the left edge through two fields for about ⅓ mile, getting views over Doulting village as you progress. A gate leads onto a track and turn left over a stile. Go down the field to the bottom left corner and cross a stile. Follow the right edge and cross a stile in the corner. Go diagonally left across the field towards St Adhelm's church, Doulting, going up and then dropping down to a stile. Once over, pass between ponds.

These were built by a member of the renowned Fussell family of Mells who had an iron works and tool edge business in Doulting.

Follow the path along and reach a stony track. Reach St Adhelm's Well on your right.

The spring emerges from the hill through a stone arch which has had two smaller arches built into it. In front is a long narrow stone-lined channel. The front part of the well is the drinking trough and up behind it is what is known as the bathing pool which may have been used by pilgrims and could have been roofed over at some stage. The well is named after St Aldhelm, the great scholar-bishop of Sherborne, who died on a visit to Doulting, the site of a fine priory, and the vigorous well of clear water was named after him from that day. One tradition about the well tells of the use of the water for religious purposes, while another emphasises the healing

Healing spring, Doulting.

qualities of the water. Over the centuries the well has kept a reputation both for sanctity and for healing, which must have led to its development as a bathing-place for pilgrims.

Follow the path uphill to the village. Before you reach the top turn right up a walled path which leads to the church of St Aldhelm's, a fine building, although rather dark, but the glorious coloured kneelers make it feel brighter.

The stone used for the church is oolitic limestone from local quarries – the same stone used in Wells Cathedral and Glastonbury Abbey.

Turn right from the church, passing the old village pump set into the wall on the right, and come to the main road with Abbey Barn Inn opposite. Turn left back to where you began.

- Abbey Barn Inn, Doulting, tel: 01749 880321.
- Strode Arms, Cranmore, tel: 01749 880450.
- The Poachers Pocket, Chelynch, tel: 01749 880220.

Circle from the Castle

Nunney – Whatley – Nunney

Distance: About 3.75 miles.
Duration: Two hours walking.
Map: OS Explorer Map 142.   Shepton Mallet and Mendip Hills East.
Reference: 735 457.

*Short on miles but full on variety! This easy circle, great for a morning
or afternoon, takes in a castle, wooded combe and open East Mendip
farmland. It has a very different feel from the high land of the Area of
Outstanding Natural Beauty in the West. The castle is fascinating, the
combe is full of wildlife alongside the stream and the farmland offers
space and peace. It is also virtually flat but there are a lot of
stiles and gates to negotiate.*

Go to Nunney village, just off the A361 south west of Frome. There is a
smalll two-hour parking area in the small market place by the old bridge,
but other options, too, nearby.

*This picturesque village situated on Nunney Brook and clustered around a four-
teenth century castle, was at one time an important clothing centre until the
eightteenth century. The market square harks back to the market licensed to
Nunney by the Crown in 1260.*

START
From the small market place, cross the old bridge in the direction of Mells
and Shepton Mallet and turn right down Castle Street to the fourteenth-
century four-square castle, looked after by English Heritage.

*It was built in the French style by John Delamere who spent much of his life in
France fighting alongside the Black Prince. In 1373 he was given a licence by
the king to fortify and crenellate his house at Nunney with a wall of stone and
lime and 'the aforesaid house so fortified and embattled may hold to himself and*

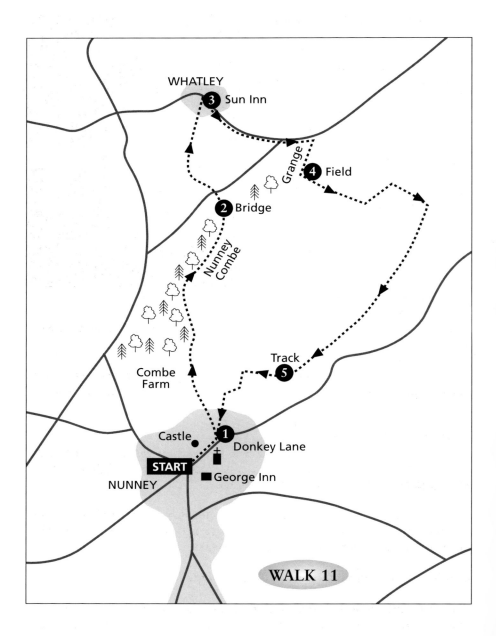

WHATLEY

3 Sun Inn

4 Field

Grange

2 Bridge

Nunney Combe

Combe Farm

Track

5

Castle

1

Donkey Lane

START

George Inn

NUNNEY

WALK 11

84

his heirs for ever without occasion or impediment...' It is said that he modelled it on the Bastille. *The castle passed by marriage in the fifteenth century to the Paulets who in Queen Elizabeth's reign sold it to the Praters. It was a Colonel Prater who defended the castle in the Civil War for the King but it fell to Fairfax who sent artillery against it in 1645. After this, it ceased to be a residence. The moat surrounding the castle is fed by an underground pipe from the brook and then it drains back into the stream.*

Walk round the moat and then cross to explore the ruins. Come out of the castle and turn left towards the church, crossing the footbridge over Nunney Brook. Turn left on the

Castle at Nunney.

main road passing the popular George, an old coaching inn, and a pretty area of the brook, a favourite spot for the very friendly ducks.

It was this spot that was used in the cloth-making days as a 'pavement and place to wash wool'. Also here is the old market cross, rescued from its fate as a garden monument in 1959.

1   DONKEY LANE
Turn left in Donkey Lane and continue to the end where, just before Combe Farm, go ahead across the grass to take the footpath on the right through a kissing gate. You are now on the Macmillan Way.

This is a 290 mile coast-to-coast long distance path from Boston in Lincolnshire to Abbotsbury in Dorset established in order to celebrate and raise money for the work of the Macmillan Cancer Relief organisation.

Continue through pretty Nunney Combe by the brook.

Wagtails dart above the stream and it's a good spot for wildflowers especially those which love water, including wood anemones, ransomes, celandine and bluebells. Unfortunately, among the plants which have taken up residence is the invasive giant hogweed.

After about ¾ mile reach a stony track.

2 BRIDGE
Go left over the bridge and follow the track up to a road. Cross and take the Macmillan Way more or less opposite, over a stile. Follow the right hedge uphill.

Just before the hedge kinks, go right through a metal kissing gate. Follow the left hedge for a few yards to the corner and then continue ahead up across the field, still climbing. At the top keep on towards a group of buildings in Whatley including a stone and tiled single storey cottage on the left end of the group. Head to the left of a house wall and go along and then over a stile or through the gate to reach the back of the Sun Inn. (Note the house nearby which has called itself 'Moon Out'!)

3 SUN INN
Turn right along the road for about seven minutes. Fortunately, it is quiet. Ignore the first lane to Nunney and continue on to a public footpath on the right. Go down the Grange and Coombe Farm drive and straight on downhill towards woodland through the car park and then through a marked gate. Go left on the track and cross the brook and follow it uphill. It sweeps around left but you continue straight ahead a few more yards and go left through a metal gate into the field on the left. There is a yellow arrow at the side. We now begin a different section of the walk through Somerset farmland – quite a change from the combe.

4 FIELD
Follow the right hedge to the very end of the field and then on through a gate and in the next field follow the left hedge. Go left over a marked stile and then ahead in the field bearing towards the far right corner, or go round the edge if there are crops.

Cross a waymarked stile on the right by the corner. Follow the left hedge. Ahead you can just see the houses on the edge of Frome. At the end of the field go over a stile and then diagonally right across this field up to a double stile. Cross and now follow the left hedge, still in the same direction as before. At the end, go left over a stile and then turn right along the right hedge. Cross a farm track and continue ahead over a stile and on still along the right hedge.

5 TRACK

Reach a stile on the right leading onto a track, probably part of the old road from Nunney to Frome. Continue along to the corner, through a kissing gate and follow the track left and all the way along and into a tarmac lane, Fulwell Lane. Go left, retracing your steps of earlier down to the main road. Turn right back into Nunney.

The church is worth a visit. Over the years it has suffered at the hands of restorers and death watch beetle, but nevertheless the various Delamere tombs are of particular interest. The founder of the castle, Sir John, lies in effigy upon the window sill in the north aisle, but behind the organ is a fifteenth-century altar tomb with a man in a tabard and Lancastrian collar and a lady in a long veil. The tomb is surrounded with coats of arms. In the north west corner is another altar tomb bearing two figures in Elizabethan costume, probably representing Richard Prater and his wife.

Continue on past, and maybe into, the George Inn – an historic old coaching inn noted for its fresh fish – and back to the start or this short but sweet circle.

℘ Inn, Whatley, tel: 01373 836219.
℘ George at Nunney, tel: 01373 836458.

Visiting the Scene of Battle

Faulkland – Norton St Philip – Hassage – Faulkland

Distance: 6.25 miles.
Duration: Approx three and a half hours walking.
Map: OS Explorer Map 142. Shepton Mallet and Mendip Hills East.
Reference: 738 544

East Mendip has a very special farmland beauty of its own – rolling country with combes, woods, streams and unique villages. The gem in this walk is the historically interesting village of Norton St Philip half way round where there are two very old beamed pubs from which to choose. It's difficult to imagine the drama and bloodshed that took place here during and after the Monmouth Rebellion. Walking is flat, except for one small hill and there are good and changing views across the open country. After heavy rain there will be wet and mud in the fields so wear good boots.

This circle begins in Faulkland a village on the A366 road between Radstock and Trowbridge, about 7 miles south of Bath. Find somewhere suitable to park.

START

By the small, picturesque village green on the eastern end of the village.

Note the stocks on the green in front of a fine old house, built by an eighteenth century eccentric, Thomas Turner.

On the opposite side of the main road, take the public footpath, past a pond and small island, built by Turner, and pretty cottages.

Faulkland was originally a mining village and many of the once humble cottages have been well restored.

Turn left on the tarmac drive and as it bends left into a stable, go straight ahead over a stile on the public footpath into a field.

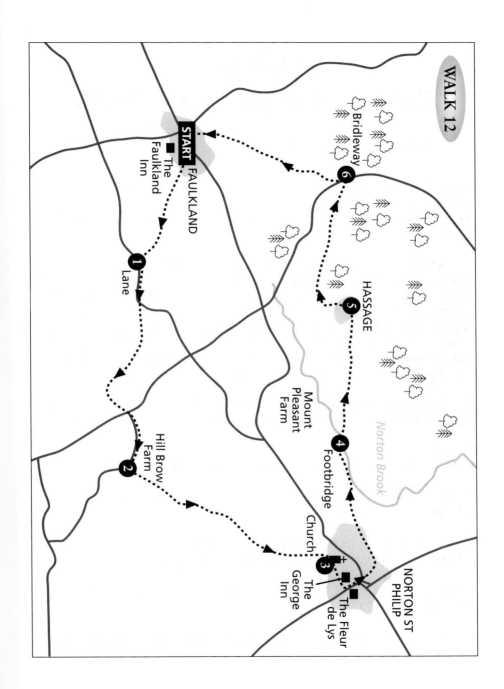

WALK 12

START FAULKLAND

The Faulkland Inn

1 Lane

Bridleway

6

5 HASSAGE

Mount Pleasant Farm

4 Footbridge

Norton Brook

2 Hill Brow Farm

Church

3

The George Inn

The Fleur de Lys

NORTON ST PHILIP

Cottages by pond at Faulkland.

Go up the left hedge/wall and at the corner continue on across the field. Already you are in open bracing country, climbing gently and getting good views across Wiltshire. Pick up a hedge on the right and follow this in the same direction. In the corner go through a double kissing gate. Continue across the next field parallel with the right edge, bearing away slightly at the end. Go through another double kissing gate. Take the footpath straight on, parallel with the right hedge, to the far side. Go through yet another kissing gate to reach a lane.

1 LANE
Turn left. Pass a farm and at the bend, go ahead on the marked bridleway. Follow this for about ¾ mile, walking along a hill edge with beautiful views. Reach a farm and go through the metal gate ahead, and then right through another gate. Turn left and pass the big barn on your left and then go round it to the left. Go through a metal gate and onto a lane.
Turn left. Take the first lane on the right after a few yards. Continue along here to a bend with Hill Brow Farm ahead.

2 FARM
Turn left on the public footpath across the field to an opening on the far side and continue on towards the right hand corner of the wood. Cross the stile

and go along with the wood on your left and continue to the corner. Cross a stile and on through fields in the same direction all the time. Start to see Norton St Philip ahead. At one point you have to go over a stream on rather inadequate stepping stones. Continue on as before. Leave the field through a barrier ahead and follow the path which leads into a better track and eventually to the village by the Old Vicarage .

In the 1086 Domesday Book, the Manor of Norton with Hinton is recorded as supporting only 20 people, 3 ploughs, a mill of 5s. rent and 20 acres of meadow. The mill had an enormous wheel, the axle measuring 10 feet in diameter and was still working within living memory.
The ruins of Hinton Priory lie 2 miles to the north of the village. The link between Norton and Hinton Priory began in 1232, when the Priory was founded. It ended on March 31st 1540 when Prior Hood and his 23 monks were evicted by the Commissioners of Henry VIII, at the time of the Dissolution of the Monastries. During the life of the Priory, the village was in the keeping of the Prior, as Lord of the Manor of Norton.
As the downland around the village was ideal for raising sheep, the Priors of Hinton Priory quickly set about expanding the wool trade and making Norton an important market for wool and cloth. It's quite likely there was some sort of market here before the founding of the Priory. Among old Somerset sayings, collected by the Folklore Society, is the statement: 'Norton were a Market Town when Taunton were a vuzzy down'. Certainly, by 1500 the parish registers contained many names described as cloth merchant or weaver. Weaving and spinning were carried on in many of the cottages, paid on a piece work basis by the cloth merchants.

Reach a small green with a seat.

Note the Gothic-style, nineteenth-century First School on the left.

Come to the main parish church.

3 CHURCH
The church is mainly perpendicular in style, of the fourteenth or fifteenth centuries and has an attractive chancel with an old barrel timber roof elaborately panelled with tracery. The east window is by Christopher Webb, famous for his stained window in Salisbury Cathedral. In the window tracery of the north wall is a little of the oldest glass in England, marked by the richness of the blues. The tower has a chiming clock without a face. Samuel Pepys visited the church and

wrote about it in his diaries. After dining at the inn, 'I walked to the church and there saw a very ancient tomb of some Knight Templar, I think; and here saw the tombstone whereon there were only two heads cut, which, the story goes, and credibly, were two sisters, called the Fair Maids of Foscott, that had two bodies upward and one belly, and there lie buried.' The ancient tomb, said by Pepys to be that of a Knight Templar, is now thought to be that of a man of law, dated from circa 1460. As for the Fair Maids, there is good reason to believe the legend, for its oddity and for the fact that the church saw fit to commemorate the sisters. Foscott is a hamlet a few miles from Norton. When Pepys saw the tomb, the effigy of the two sisters was cut in stone on the floor of the nave. This has since disappeared except for the two heads which are set on the wall inside the tower, one clearly defined and one much worn.

Go into the churchyard, pass the main door and continue on out the other side into a recreation field. Head for the far left corner where you go up a path between high stone walls to the main road. Right is the George and opposite the Fleur de Lys, both very old and welcoming inns with open fires and good food.

The George, a Grade 1 listed building, claims to be one of the oldest continuously licensed houses, offering hospitality since 1397. The licence would have been given by the Prior in those days. It may have been that, when the monks moved here to found the Priory, they first built on this spot to provide temporary living accomodation. Whatever the accuracy of the dates, it is certain that the monks built the present George Inn which was used as the guest house.

On the far side of the George is an interesting historic information board about Norton St Philip's role in the Monmouth Rebellion and the battle in the village in June 1685.

Monmouth had landed at Lyme Regis early in June with 80 men intent on gathering an army to oust his uncle, the Roman Catholic King James II. He moved triumphantly up through Somerset gathering men, having at one time about 7000. However, they were untrained and ill-armed and just outside Bristol, at Keynsham, they were defeated by the Royalists So, it was a depleted and disheartened rebel army that trailed south past Bath, hoping to gather more recruits in Wiltshire, and came to rest for the night in Norton. Monmouth made the George Inn his headquarters, with billets being sought for his men, and stables for the horses, throughout the village. Norton effectively became an armed camp for the night.

As Monmouth prepared to leave next day, news came of the approaching advance guard of the Royalist Army and this experienced commander decided to stand and fight, setting up a strong barricade in the main street, North Street. After several hours, the Royalists withdrew having lost 80 men. The rebels lost only 18. However, once the rebellion was finally put down, the battle and defeat in Norton was not forgotten. Men from the village were taken to the Assize Court at Wells. Some were transported, fined or flogged, and 12 were brought back to the village and hanged in Bloody Close, behind the Fleur de Lys. Their bodies were then hung about the village, until taken down, burnt and buried in field behind the Fleur.

Apart from its role in the rebellion, another much more recent claim to fame for the George is its use as a location for films including Tom Jones *and* Pride and Prejudice.

Across the road from the George, the Fleur de Lys may be nearly as old as the George itself and is named after the original owner, a very rich landowner in the area in the sixteenth century, Geoffrey Flower. He farmed 735 acres and gave generously to the reconstruction of the church as well as being largely responsible for the rebuilding of Bath Abbey.

The Fleur was opened as an inn in 1584. Not long afterwards, in 1615, Queen Anne of Denmark, wife of James I, stopped here to dine on her way back from taking the waters at Bath. Dinner for herself and her retinue cost £2 13s 0d. Samuel Pepys, his wife and maid, also dined here on their way to Bath in 1668. Their bill was 10s 0d.

If you have time, it's worth exploring some of the village which has come through the centuries still retaining much of its original character. Many cottages still have mullioned windows, stone-tiled roofs and local stone facings. Many of the place names were in use during Henry VIII's time.

Go down the road towards Radstock and Wells opposite the Fleur de Lys and to the side of the George – just for a few yards. This is the start of Bell Hill which has an interesting history.

Down the hill, where the garage is now, stood the Prince Blucher Inn. The heavy wagons, particularly the coal wagons from Radstock, were defeated by the hill without extra help. So a rope ran from the inn all the way up the hill to end in a bell which rang in a stable in the courtyard of the George – hence the name of the hill. In the stable was a cart-horse whose job it was, on hearing the bell, to go down the hill, entirely on its own, and help the wagon up to level ground at the top. It would there be unhitched, a small sum of money would be placed in a leather pouch at its head, and the horse would go back to its stable, again quite unsupervised. It seems unclear when this arrangement began but it was certainly still going within living memory.

Cross and go right along North Street (mentioned earlier as the centre of most of the fighting between Monmouth and the Royalists) and at the junction turn left down hill to reach a triangle of grass at Lyde Green.

Lyde Green may have been the earliest part of the village and the grassy triangle is the only remaining common land in the village.

To see the unique Tudor Dovecote, go left for about 60 yards up the lane and it is set back on the right up a short drive.

The Dovecot, is likely to have been built by the monks as part of the Manor Farm complex, which also had a private chapel. The dovecot is one of the finest examples of its sort in the UK and was restored in the 1970s. There are 800 pigeon holes in total. The reason, of course, for dovecots in those days can be given briefly as 'pigeon pie when you wanted it', for the household of the Lord of the Manor. Farmers thought of pigeons as pests and weren't too keen on the idea of dovecots.

To continue, go straight across at Lyde Green down Ringwell Lane. Just past the bend, turn right on the right of way towards Hassage and follow it for about ¾ mile. Now, ahead of you, lording it from above is Mount Pleasant farm. Here the track bends right and crosses Norton Brook over a wooden footbridge.

4 FOOTBRIDGE
Once over, follow the track through a gate and uphill. Come up into a field and follow the right edge. Go through another gate and continue up to the top – in the same direction all the time. The track reaches a wall/hedge ahead and bends gently left. Pass a ruined farm building and look down on the valley below. Join a stony track and go ahead, dropping downhill into the tiny hamlet of Hassage.

5 HASSAGE
Turn left up the lane past Hassage Manor. Go round a left bend and then at the right bend, go up steps over a stile on the right. Head across to the woodland corner on the far side. Follow the wood on your right. Reach a gate, which you may have to climb if locked. Continue on with the wood

still on your right and as it ends continue ahead across the field in the same direction and through an opening in the hedge near the end. Continue on towards a stile barrier ahead. Cross this (watch the barbed wire tucked under the top rail) and go ahead through a narrow strip of field and over a stile by woodland. Continue on, as before, with the main woodland on your right through a newer oak plantation on a not terribly clear path. At the corner go left a few yards and through the barrier (which may be wire) into a field.

Turn right and follow the wood on your right. When it ends, continue on, heading towards a house up ahead. You now go straight ahead up through three fields and two gates keeping to the right below the house. You will probably be greeted by loud barking from the dogs in kennels at the house. Head for the far top corner of the last field, which had two horses in it when I came through. They were interested in my dog and needed a few stern shouts. Cross the stile barrier onto a lane. Turn left.

After a few yards go right on the public bridleway.

6 BRIDLEWAY

Go up into the field diagonally left and along the top. Then bear right down the other side to a wooden hunting gate below by a large oak. Go through the gate and follow the track for about a mile into Faulkland, bending round the edge of fields, and getting fresh views en route. Go left on a small lane to reach the main road in Faulkland opposite the Faulkland Inn.

Norton St Philip:
❧ The George Inn, tel: 01373 834861.
❧ The Fleur de Lys, tel: 01373 834333.

Faulkland:
❧ The Faulkland Inn, tel: 01373 834312.

REFERENCE MATERIAL

The Heart of Mendip, F. A. Knight, Chatford House Press
Old Mendip, Robin Atthill, David & Charles
Mendip, a New Study, Robin Atthill, David & Charles
The Mendips, Coysh, Manson and Waite, Robert Hale Ltd
The Somerset Landscape, Michael Havinden, Hodder & Stoughton
Some Buildings of Mendip, R. D. Reid, The Mendip Society
The Mendips, Robin and Romey Williams Ex Libris Press
The Book of Somerset Villages, Sheila Bird, Dovecote Press
The King's England, Somerset, Arthur Mee, Hodder & Stoughton